Wisdom of the
GUIDES

Rocky Mountain Trout Guides
Talk Fly Fishing

Paul Arnold

Photographs by the author

Frank
Amato
PUBLICATIONS, INC.

Published in 1998 by
Frank Amato Publications, Inc.
PO Box 82112
Portland, Oregon 97282
(503) 653-8108

Hardbound ISBN: 1-57188-128-X
Hardbound UPC: 0-66066-00327-0

All photographs taken by the author.
Dust jacket: Amy Tomlinson
Book Design: Tony Amato

Printed in the United States

1 3 5 7 9 10 8 6 4 2

Contents

Introduction..5

Gary LaFontaine
(Deer Lodge, Montana)...6

Craig Mathews
(West Yellowstone, Montana)...29

Johnny Gomez
(Navajo Dam, New Mexico)..40

Thomas J. Knopick and John W. Flick
(Durango, Colorado)..54

Jennifer Olsson
(Bozeman, Montana)..65

Larry Tullis
(Salt Lake City, Utah)...78

Mike Lawson
(Island Park, Idaho)...92

Charlie Gilman
(Hotchkiss, Colorado)..104

Al Troth
(Dillon, Montana)...118

Paul Roos
(Helena, Montana)...134

Dedication

Dedicated to my Granddad, Albert W. Funkhouser.
As mentor and wayshower, he opened the doors to fishing,
hunting and all the outdoors for me.

Introduction

It is perhaps best that this book be put together by an average fisherman like me. I am in awe of the knowledge and skills of guides. I hope that my respect and admiration—as well as their knowledge and skill—show through in these pages.

The interviews included here represent only about a third of the guides I interviewed. In every case, the guides who are absent were left out because of the limitations of space or geographic considerations, or both. For example, interviews of the guides of Dillon, Montana—near both the Big Hole and the Beaverhead rivers—could constitute a book unto themselves, but only one of them is included here.

I thank every guide who gave of his or her time and energy to talk to me and my tape recorder, whether or not they appear in this book. Each of you has earned not only my appreciation, but also my acknowledgment that without you, this book could not and would not be.

Gary LaFontaine

Where to reach him:

P.O. Box 166

Deer Lodge, Montana 59722

Phone: 406/846-3876

Professionally guides now: No

Homewaters: Rivers, lakes and streams of southwestern Montana

Born: Connecticut, 1945

Came West: 1963, 18 years old. Came to Montana for college at University of Montana and stayed after graduation.

Guiding history: Guided professionally for eight years in Montana, principally the Madison and Big Hole rivers. Stopped guiding professionally in the early '80s. Recreational guide now.

Publications and videos:

Challenge of the Trout, Mountain Press Publishing (1976);

Caddisflies, Lyons & Burford (1981);

The Dry Fly: New Angles, Greycliff Publishing Co. (1990);

Trout Flies: Proven Patterns, Greycliff Publishing Co. (1993).

Featured in the videos "Tying and Fishing Caddisflies" (The Jack Dennis Fly Fishing Video Library) and "Successful Fly Fishing Strategies," Volumes I and II (Miracle Productions).

Gary and I conducted our interviewing session in the living room of his house on a quiet, residential street in Deer Lodge, Montana. He lives alone, except for his dogs, and his home has that relaxed look of a place not tended by woman; fly fishing and tying paraphernalia is lying about and stacks of "The Book Mailer," the book catalogue that Gary writes and distributes, were stacked in the living and dining rooms awaiting mailing.

When we began the interview we weren't working alone. Gary's Rottweiler, Zeb, was there with us, but after Zeb knocked my tape recorder off the coffee table a couple of times, Gary ushered him out the door to the front porch. After that things went smoothly.

We talked together for more than three hours; our interview was relaxed and unhurried. The LaFontaine persona you see on those videos with Dick Sharon, "Trout Fishing Strategies," was the same person answering my questions. That is to say, in person as well as before a camera Gary is a genuinely funny guy who can't help projecting enthusiasm for fly fishing and the outdoors. Also, he has a high degree of that quality common to most good guides—the gift and enjoyment of teaching. When I left I not only knew I'd gotten a good interview, I'd learned some things about fly fishing for trout and been entertained as well.

Question: When did you start guiding?
LaFontaine: When I grew up I used to guide in Georgia. That was when I was nine years old during summer vacations with the family. I guided in the swamps for bass in the Okefenokee for $15 a day. I had my little motor boat and I'd take people into the swamp to fish. The barber in town sent me quite a bit of business. Later, when I grew up a bit, I guided some in Connecticut, too. On Wonoscopomuc Lake. That's a good trout lake up in the northwest corner of the state.

I did my serious professional guiding in Montana, on the Madison and the Big Hole.

Q: Are your guiding days over?
LaFontaine: I don't guide professionally anymore, but I'm sure a recreational guide. When I go out with friends the first thing I want to do is to make sure that they catch fish. I'm under the same kind of mindset then as when I was guiding. So, in effect, I'm still guiding but not for money.

Good Clients

Q: Speaking as a professional guide, what is your favorite kind of client?
LaFontaine: I have people ask me, "Gee, don't you hate taking out beginners?" No, I love taking out beginners because of their enthusiasm and because you're helping them. And I love taking out experienced anglers, too.

I especially like to guide a client who loves to fish, loves to be outdoors. I don't care if they're a good fisherman, but I like to guide someone who is going to be excited about the experience.

Q: Does that kind of person fall into any particular category, such as age, gender, social class, etc.?
LaFontaine: I've had everyone from eight-year-old boys to eighty-year-old women who've been in that class, who just loved the experience and were excited about it.

Q: Do you think that guides are more important on some waters than on others?
LaFontaine: Definitely so. Some rivers are pretty predictable and pretty easy and I don't know how much you need to have a guide for that. But on the Big Hole, which is such a tremendously fickle river, a guide is worth his weight in gold because he has the up-to-date information on the hatches, he knows where the fish are at that time and when they're going to turn on. The difference between having a good guide and a bad guide on the Big Hole is the difference between catching 20 fish, a lot of them nice ones, and catching zero. I've seen so many people skunked there.

Good Guides

Q: What are some of the qualities that make a good guide?
LaFontaine: Some people should never guide. Some people should always guide. I think that the basis of it is liking people.

As a guide, you're a psychologist. You have to start off with the idea that you have to find the buttons that are going to make these people have an enjoyable day. If that means showing them the insects, if that means explaining the history of the area, talking about the flowers or pointing out the species of birds going around, that's all part of being a guide. You are not just there for the fishing; you are a host. You're also a representative of that river, and if you don't love the river and can't portray that love to these people then you've lost something there too.

So guiding is not just catching fish. It's the entire interaction between humans.

Q: When you guide a fisherman, exactly what are you trying to accomplish?
LaFontaine: If I can take someone for two or three days I don't just want to affect his fishing for those two or three days. I want to teach him new methods, I want to introduce him to new flies. I want to change the way he's going to fly fish forever. I'm going to change the way he approaches fish, the way he casts and gets dead-drift floats to fish. I want to change the patterns he uses, the

methods he uses. I'm even going to change the clothes he wears. I want to change his whole focus of fly fishing and life in general. He's going to go back a different man. His wife isn't going to know who he is.

And I think that's what a good guide does. He's like any teacher in that his impact goes far beyond the time he spends with a student.

Gary as Client

Q: How do you, yourself, approach being a client rather than a guide when you go to a new fishing area?

LaFontaine: I listen to the guide. That's maybe the most important advice that I can give anybody. When I go to someplace new I do exactly what the guide says. I don't come in and tell him I want to try my way, this fly or that technique. I'll do those things afterwards, after I've learned what's going on and seen the river and done exactly what I've been told to do.

My advice to clients is not only to do what the guide says to do, but to question him and ask him exactly why he does what he does. And that's the way you learn new things.

And from the standpoint of my advice to guides, I'd say to be a little bit more flexible and open. It's surprising how much you can learn from your clients.

A Poaching Client

Q: What's your least favorite kind of client?

LaFontaine: Definitely the hard-driving types who consider the fish as an object is my least favorite client. Let me tell you a quick story. It's fairly well known around West Yellowstone.

I was guiding on the Madison. I guided there for four years. In all my years of guiding I've only had two bad clients. I *love* to be with people. One of these two bad clients came in, told me his name (let's say his first name was Stephan), and said, "I'm hiring you to be my guide today. I learned to be a world-class skier in one year, and I'm going to be a world-class fisherman in one year." I didn't like that. Then he has to take me out to his van and show me a cooler full of dead fish.

I told him I'd planned to take him to Yellowstone Park because there are plenty of fish, but you can't kill any fish in there and you obviously want to kill fish. Then I tell him that the fish there are in the 20-inch class, we'll have rising fish and it's a great classroom. So he says OK, we'll go to Yellowstone.

When we get to Yellowstone he's mad because I'm switching back and forth between him and his wife, and his wife has caught a 20-inch fish and he hasn't. If it was my wife I'd have been tickled pink, but he was jealous. I keep going back and forth between them and I come back to him and he is gutting a trout.

I say, "What are you doing?" He says, "Oh, I just had to keep one to show people."

"You can't do that," I tell him. He says, "Just one."

"Look, Stephan," I say to him, "it's obvious you want to keep fish so let me take you someplace where you can catch a lot of fish and keep them all. But we have to leave here." He says OK, but asks if he should keep the fish he gutted. I tell him, "Definitely yes, just put it in your cooler." He puts it in his cooler. I'm driving and the cooler's in the back of my truck.

We're driving out and we get to the gate, and I stop. I get out of the truck and walk over to the ranger, point at Stephan and say, "I'm turning that man in. He killed a cutthroat on the Yellowstone River."

Stephan jumps out and he's trying to get to me. Two rangers are holding him back, their feet skidding and he's screaming and yelling. His wife was a nice lady and she was sitting in the truck trying to hold back a laugh. Finally, there was a gap in the screaming and yelling, and I looked at him and said, "Stephan, does this mean I don't get a tip?"

His wife cracks up, she couldn't take it any longer. I don't know if they stayed married after that. But that is the client I dislike the most. I hate that kind of client.

I don't mind someone being intense. I'm intense. I really want to catch fish. But that doesn't mean that I sit here with a clicker saying 28, 29, 30 trout, and measuring every one and quantifying the experience.

Common Fishing Mistakes

Q: What are common fishing errors that non-expert fishermen make?
LaFontaine: I'll tell you, it's the people who are experts who make the mistakes.

I don't know how many times I've had a husband and wife fishing together when he's done a lot of fishing and she fishes just sort of haphazardly. She's usually in the back of the boat and he's in the front. He'll make these perfect straight line casts, tight line, lay that line out there perfect. And he'll have microdrag that he can't see from the boat.

The wife is sitting in back, she'll flop the line out there and it's all curls in the water, doesn't go anywhere near any particular structure. It's just drifting along. She outfishes him two to one. On dry flies I've had that happen consistently. That was a rule, not an exception.

The big error most people make from a boat (and I think they probably do the same thing when they're wading) is they don't put enough slack out there to get a drag-free presentation. They have microdrag. They don't get a good, long drift. If you're good in that boat, putting slack in the line to start out with and mending as you're going along, then you can get a 40- or 50-foot drift. Especially if the boatman is good and isn't constantly wagging the boat around.

10

So being able to cast too well can be a disadvantage. It's simple efficiency. The more your fly's in the water the better your chance to catch trout.

Tackle Selection

Q: What about tackle and equipment that people show up with? Do they make mistakes in their purchases?

LaFontaine: Twenty years ago you used to see a lot of bad mistakes. People would come out with mis-matched outfits, grandpa's old rod, worn out line and things like that. Now every rod company out there is making great rods. It's very hard to buy a bad rod. All the lines are great, the leaders are pre-tapered.

If anything, these days, especially for wade fishing, people often bring too heavy a rod. Most of them come out with a six- or seven-weight and you don't need that. My main rod is a Sage 389 LL. That's what I use for all my shallow-water nymphing and dry-fly fishing. It's an 8'9" in a three-weight. I like a slow rod. There are good rods from other good companies, too. Like a Scott four-weight. I'm not aligned with Sage, or anybody else, incidentally.

A lot of time with spooky fish the lighter line and more delicate presentation is going to be an advantage. So if anything I would say to bring a lighter rod. Bring the heavy rod for the boat fishing and for the heavy nymph fishing, but don't be afraid to bring your three-weight or two-weight along.

Q: What about different types of drag on reels here in Montana?

LaFontaine: Where you need an exceptional drag, as good as any drag you'd need on saltwater, is for very light-tippet midge fishing. The reason is that a bad drag will have a catch-and-go action that will break off the fly. Whereas a great drag is very smooth and sort of feeds it out. That keeps the fish from overrunning, keeps the fish tired out and helps you play him.

So a good drag is very essential with light tippets.

Observe Before You Fish

Q: If you could require your clients to follow a few basic fishing rules to improve their fishing, what would they be?

LaFontaine: Rule number one for catching more fish is to stop and look. What happens with people is that when they come out West to fish they're so excited that they want to rush into the water. They splash out through the fish.

Fish feed in very, very shallow water. They feed at the lips of pools, they feed on the little gravel shelf coming in on the shallow side and they snub up right close to the bank. And when people step into the water and spook fish, they've spooked not only those fish but wherever those fish are running to. If you've got a nervous, scared fish that runs up into another area, then those fish pick up on that and they're nervous and scared too.

The first thing I do to help people catch more fish is to teach them how to stop and watch a stream for ten minutes before they start casting. A guide walks up and says OK, do so-and-so. That's because he's been there yesterday and the day before. If I go to a strange piece of water I will sit down and I will just watch. It's amazing how much you can see before you start fishing. That ten minutes is going to set the tone for the whole day.

Q: What are you looking for?
LaFontaine: What I'm looking for are fish, or signs of fish. I'm studying the water, I'm studying the insects to see what's coming off the surface and then I'm looking for actual fish. That could be either fish flashing down deep or rising or even moving.

Nymphing At Sunrise

Q: What other rules would you have them follow?
LaFontaine: This is a really important rule. In July and August when the weather is warm the good nymph fishing is early in the morning at dawn. How many times have you heard that you don't need to get up early, that trout fishing is gentleman fishing and the good fishing doesn't start until 10 or 11 o'clock in the morning? You've probably heard that a thousand times, right? It's always wrong.

The best time of the day during warm weather, always—every time—is at dawn. And that's because when there is a shift of the light you get something called behavioral drift. That's where the insects are going back into cover. They're moving around, they break away and they drift free in the current. You do studies and you see the big spike of the insects going free in the drift. It's not the amount of insects that determine the feeding patterns of trout; it's the amount of insects that are vulnerable. And the insects are vulnerable when they're drifting free at dawn when there is a shift in the light.

Dawn isn't a good dry-fly time, typically. But it's a great nymphing time. So when people are out here in July and August, if they'll go out at dawn and fish nymphs through that first crack of light, then go back and have breakfast or take a nap, they'll have some of the most spectacular fishing of the trip, the biggest fish and the most fish. And that's true not just in the West, but everywhere.

Q: Anything else on the rules for better fishing?
LaFontaine: Stealth. Learn how to creep up on the fish. Don't spook 'em. Bend down, wear dark clothes, don't stomp on the ground—those are the basic rules.

Sort of related to that is avoiding the pressure of other fishermen, particularly guide boats. You want to give the river at least a two-hour rest. You don't want to be fishing water that's been pounded by every boat going through. And when you're wade fishing it's real easy to do that. In the morning you fish where they're going to end up and in the evening you fish where they started out.

Landing Fish

Q: What do you teach people about how to land the fish they've hooked?

LaFontaine: We work with clients on landing fish and getting them in pretty quickly. Often you'll see people bring a fish in close then the fish will take off and make another run, and this will happen three or four times. You can usually take that fish the first time you bring him in if you make the rod go whip, whip, whip—making an arc with the rod. It turns the fish over and it's like turning over an alligator; the sudden movement disorients them. Doing this, you can get him in the first time and take him. That way the fish is still fresh and doesn't have any lactic acid buildup in his muscles. Unhook him, slide him out and he swims away.

Principles of Fly Selection

Q: I want to ask you some questions about your own fishing techniques, and with you that's heavy-duty stuff because of your expertise and the all the books you've written.

LaFontaine: Not much expertise, and I only write books because it keeps me out of bars in the winter.

Q: Most people who've fished for a while end up in one of two categories; either having a vest full of a lot of fly patterns or carrying just a few favorite patterns. Which category are you in?

LaFontaine: I'm in the extreme end of having a lot of patterns with me, and using them.

Q: What's your reason for that?

LaFontaine: It's real simple. There's only one reason to fish and that's to have fun. And for me it's fun to carry a lot of flies and to experiment. If someone came up with a fly and said, "Here, this is all you'll ever need," it would ruin a lot of my enjoyment.

That doesn't mean that you can't get away with two or three general flies, but the guy who fishes like that learns to avoid tough situations. He doesn't go to the Missouri when the fish are sipping on Trico spinners. And the pods of fish are up there and there are thousands of insects, and the rising fish are going blip, blip, blip. He doesn't go there and fish his Royal Wulff. He may do it and even catch an occasional fish, but he's not going to consistently catch fish. So he's going to avoid those situations. He's going to go out at a time of day when the insects aren't heavy, on a stream with a riffle where he has a better chance.

I don't want to avoid those tough situations. To me, those are the ones I love. And so therefore I want to specifically have a size 18 Trico spinner with an olive thorax and a washed-out cream body.

That's what my book *Trout Flies* [Greycliff Publishing Co. (1993)] is all about, it's a system. If you carry the full range of flies in your box then you can meet every specific situation.

Role of Entomology

Q: Where does entomology fit into all that?

LaFontaine: Most people have the completely wrong idea about entomology. "It's too tough, it's too confusing, it makes it too difficult."

I can go out to the Clark Fork with one fly pattern. Just let me tie it up the night before. How can I do that? Because I know exactly what's going to be hatching. I know exactly what the fish are going to be feeding on and I know what time they're going to start rising. It's all because of the study of entomology.

And that's what entomology does; it allows you to simplify the choice of flies you carry along. But, I want that very, very specific fly. I don't want a general fly.

Q: What I'm hearing is that on any given day you may not carry a large number of patterns, but that will be because you have already selected, from a large number of patterns, the specific flies you'll want to use that day. Is that a fair summary?

LaFontaine: Absolutely correct. And the key to that is the study of entomology. It allows me to simplify my approach.

Theory of Color Attraction

Q: Is there any principle other than knowledge of entomology that might govern the selection of patterns?

LaFontaine: There sure is. It's the theory of color attraction and I describe it in my book *The Dry Fly* [Greycliff Publishing Co. (1990)]. Basically the theory is that you use a fly having the same color as the color of the light in which you're fishing because the color of that fly will be intensified by that light.

I know a lot of guides, as you might guess, and a lot of their clients refuse to fish anything but dry flies. They won't fish nymphs or streamers or anything other than dry flies. When nothing is happening by way of hatches they use general attractors and the guides say that following the theory of color attraction has increased their catch rates by 20 to 30 percent.

The theory is really quite simple and is based on the fact that, as every photographer knows, light has color. In the evening it might be orange, during the day it might be yellowish green and kind of bluish in the shade. If you match the color of the fly to the color of the light it will look intense. The reason is that if you have a red fly all the colors of the light are absorbed except red, and that's bounced out. Obviously, if you're using that red fly in the evening when you have red light there's more red light hitting that red fly and therefore it looks on fire. The physics of it are very simple but it has been an incredible boost. For instance, the advice to use a gray fly on a gray day is the oldest axiom in fly fishing. The theory of color attraction explains why it works.

I've seen the theory work so many times. It's such a powerful, powerful theory. To me, in guiding, if a guide is not following that very simple theory of color attraction—if he hasn't studied it, hasn't learned it, and if he's not carrying a selection of patterns to meet it—then he's really doing his clients a disservice. It makes that much of a difference.

Q: That theory applies only to dry-fly attractor patterns though, doesn't it?
LaFontaine: Exactly. When you're matching, you match the color of the insect on the water.

Nymphs are entirely different. As soon as you get underwater then you're working on a whole different rule of physics. Under the water you get involved with light filtration, certain colors not going to certain depths and other factors.

There we develop nymphs like the Teardrop that have just a little bit of fluorescence in them, just enough to attract the fish. So there is a theory of attraction for nymphs, but it's different. And that theory isn't fully formed in my mind yet.

Q: How about using fluorescent colors in dry flies?
LaFontaine: We've found that you have to be real careful with fluorescence on the surface. You shouldn't overuse it. We dye an orange hackle fluorescent in one of our patterns, then we wind it with a brown hackle.

Q: Fly shops are full of parachute patterns with posts of fluorescent red, pink and lime green. How do you feel about that?
LaFontaine: I don't think it makes any difference in the way the fly fishes except that it makes it easier for the fisherman to see, which is always the key.

Nymphing
Q: You're talking a lot about dry flies, and you've written a book about them. Do you enjoy nymphing as much as you enjoy fishing dry flies?

LaFontaine: Yes. And no. I really, really enjoy shallow-water nymph fishing. In other words where you're spotting fish and casting to them. It's a very visual game. Or even fishing nymphs with an indicator where the fish are just a few feet under the surface. I do not enjoy deep, blind nymph fishing as much. I do enjoy it, but I'm not particularly good at it.

My friend Dick Sharon is a master at that. Two nymphs, two very tiny nymphs. Fished very deep. I call it tid-bit fishing.

The reason I'm not as good at it is because I have such a strong preference for dry fly and shallow-water nymphing. If I had to use deep nymphs, I'd use deep nymphs, but given a choice I won't. If I'm fishing deep and see a fish rise—I don't care if it's a six-inch trout—off goes the nymph, off goes the lead, on goes a dry fly and then I start fishing that. So because of my strong preference I don't use deep-nymph methods as a foundation, which is what you should do, and therefore I'm not incredibly good at it. I can get good if I work at it day after day.

Q: Do you ever nymph fish without a strike indicator?
LaFontaine: Oh yes. Just simple sight fishing, sure. But I use an indicator for deep nymphing and even for certain shallow-water nymphing. My favorite line about deep-water nymphing is from Mike Lawson. He said, "I'd rather watch snow melt than blind-fish a nymph." That doesn't apply to me but it applies to him. I love that line, you know.

The whole thing about fly fishing is that it's supposed to be fun. If you have more fun not catching fish on a dry fly than catching fish on a deep nymph, then fish a dry fly. And there are people who are like that.

Gary's Favorite Patterns
Q: Even though you use a lot of patterns, do you have some favorite dry-fly patterns that you generally rely on?
LaFontaine: Oh, I think I'm like everybody else on that. In spite of the fact that I carry a lot of flies there are ones that I use over and over.

Q: What are some of those flies?
LaFontaine: I can name a few flies that I think anybody coming out West to fish should have available.

Gotta have the Mohawk. The Mohawk is a good fly in its own right. It looks like a little beetle. It's a wedge of cork with a little chunk of deer hair that sinks 3/4 of the way below the surface.

Q: That's one you designed, isn't it?
LaFontaine: That's one my daughter designed, actually. The thing that's so

great about the Mohawk is not just fishing it by itself, but it is the perfect strike indicator. A lot of people now are fishing two dry patterns by tying on about nine inches of monofilament to the eye of the first fly.

I like to tie from the eye rather than tying off the bend of the hook because I think that it's harder to hook a fish on a fly with leader coming off the bend. It costs you strikes. The leader gets in the way, I think. Anyway, tying off of the eye works better for me. But the reason for nine inches is that if it's longer the fish can take the back fly and you might not see the strike. Whereas with nine inches you're not depending so much on the fly to move; you see the swirl right near the fly. So you just strike on the visual indication of a take.

A lot of people are fishing a combination like a Mohawk and an emerger pattern, an emerger pattern being half in and half out of the film. We're all getting older, it's all getting tough to see. I don't need to see the emerger; that Mohawk is going to tell me where the fly is all the time. It's a great little indicator pattern.

So I'd say to make sure you have the Mohawk. Very visible, plus it's a beetle and I have a friend who's been catching fish with it on the Letort, and that's one of the toughest spring creeks going.

The Double Wing

Q: What other favorite patterns?
LaFontaine: Number two, I'd say you want the Double Wing. The Double Wing is a fly that's geared to the color theory of attraction. There are four or five main colors. If you have four colors in various sizes then you'd be ready to fish attractors whenever the trout weren't actually feeding on insects.

Q: That's not a real common pattern. Tell me about it.
LaFontaine: It's getting common. When the book *Caddisflies* [Lyons & Burford (1981)] came out it took about eight years for the Emergent Sparkle Pupa to catch on. The Emergent Sparkle Pupa is now one of the more popular commercial flies in the country.

The Double Wing is very fast becoming that way because it's geared to that theory of attraction. Because people who use the color theory of attraction catch a lot of fish.

Q: Why is it called a Double Wing?
LaFontaine: It has two wings.

Q: A Royal Wulff has two wings. Does the Double Wing have a total of four?
LaFontaine: No, no, no. This is a down-wing pattern. There are two down wings. *[Gary hands a fly to the interviewer]* Here is a Double Wing.

17

Not a Trude

Q: It looks like a Trude.

LaFontaine: Yeah, but it's not when you look at it from the bottom. That's the difference. See, here is the underwing, which is yellow on this one. Then the body and the hot spot of sparkle yarn so when you look at it from the bottom you don't see that top wing of kip tail; that's for the fisherman.

Plus, when there is light coming down, especially in the evening, when it comes down at an angle, then it hits the water and bounces up. Well when the light hits that white kip tail it reflects back down and maximizes the light and creates that hot spot. It has the same general shape as a Trude, but totally different when looking up from the bottom. This fly utilizes the theory of color attraction with the colored wing, with the tuft of sparkle yarn which is the tail, and with the body color.

The Double Wing is visible because on the top it has kip tail. But from the bottom you don't see that kip tail. Every aspect of that fly is designed to attract fish because of the hot spot of color. So if you're using the orange Double Wing in the evening, the orange is maximized. If you use the lime one during the middle of the day, or use it around vegetation where there's a lot of reflected green, then the green is maximized. Same thing with the white, same thing with the pink. This is the fly that utilizes the theory of color attraction I was talking about earlier.

Emergent Sparkle Pupa

Q: So the Mohawk is one of the flies you'd recommend and another is the Double Wing. What are some others?

LaFontaine: I'd have to keep the Emergent Sparkle Pupa high on the list. I mean one of the most frustrating things in the world is to see people come out here and not have the emerger. Selectivity, when it happens, is important. Fish are selective to color and size, but the thing they're most selective about is brightness. When the insect has brightness the fly has to have brightness. If it doesn't, you're not going to catch them. The Emergent, with the Antron yarn, has that brightness.

Q: In your book Caddisflies *you have a large number of colors for your emergers. Reading the book I get the impression you're suggesting that a person should have all those colors available to get the full effectiveness of that pattern. Is that a correct interpretation?*

LaFontaine: Four color combinations will cover 90 percent of the situations with the emerger patterns. Now, when I describe these color combinations the first word refers to the deer hair wing and the second word refers to the underbody and overbody. The four combinations are: brown/yellow, brown/bright green, gray/gray and ginger/ginger.

18

Q: Your emerger patterns have been pretty well accepted, haven't they?

LaFontaine: They have, as a matter of fact. I heard a good story about that the other day. A guy wrote me from Oregon to tell it to me. He and a couple of his buddies from Oregon had gone to fish the Beaverkill. They knew each other from work, but had never fished together. "The first day," he wrote, "one of the other guys was catching fish but I wasn't catching any fish. I asked him, 'What do I need?' The answer was, 'You need ESP.' " The guy who wrote said he was discouraged because he'd never had any particular powers like that.

This went on for two more days. The one guy kept catching fish and every time the guy who wrote to me asked him what he was using he said, "ESP." So on the last day, with the same guy catching all the fish, the guy who wrote me said, "I guess you just have to have ESP." And the other guy said, "Yeah, if you don't have the Emergent Sparkle Pupa, you're not going to catch any of these fish."

That fly makes more difference between success and failure than any other fly I've ever seen. And it's because of the brightness. It's awful to see people come out here and the fish are jumping all around, but they're unable to catch a fish because a dry fly doesn't work, no matter how good the dry fly. The fish are taking that pupa, half in and half out of the film. So you take a Mohawk and dangle a pupa back off of it.

Q: Do you ever fish the pupa alone, without a dry as an indicator?

LaFontaine: Yes, on flat water, and I grease the pupa. Body, wing, everything. But on rougher water it's awfully hard to see, even greased. It's flush to the water. So on that kind of water I generally use the Mohawk as an indicator.

Q: What other top-water flies do you like?

LaFontaine: As a guide, I like to let people use their own flies. I learn a lot from that. I try to adapt to what they have in their boxes. Then if they don't work we go to the ones that I've already mentioned. Those are pretty much my favorites.

Bead Head Twist Nymph

Q: What nymphs do you like to use?

LaFontaine: First, the Bead Head Twist Nymph. It uses a tying technique that creates a great effect under water.

Q: Is that described in one of your books?

LaFontaine: Yeah, it's in *Trout Flies. [Interviewer's note: Here Gary sets up a vise on his coffee table, grabs a portable tying material kit, and begins to tie a Bead Head Twist Nymph. As he ties, he talks.]* When you're as bad a fly tier as

19

I am you need to know every trick you can use. Basically, I taught myself how to tie flies when I was about nine years old.

Now I'm going to do some dubbing here. I use a method I call touch-dubbing. I chop the dubbing up real fine, about 3/16 of an inch *then* churn it up in the blender. No commercial dubbing is this fine.

For touch-dubbing, first you wax the thread. I use Wonder Wax, but it isn't made anymore. B.T.'s Super Tacky and Loon's Hi-Tack are modern substitutes. After you get the thread waxed, you just touch the dubbing to the thread. Just like patting your cheeks.

This dubbing is Antron yarn. Most material is neutral; it gives shape, color, or size but there's no inherent magic within the material itself. But some materials do have inherent magic. One of those materials is peacock herl, because of its iridescence. Another material, a synthetic, with inherent magic is Antron yarn. What if you could combine the magic of the two without detracting from the magic of either one? Then you'd have double magic. And the only way to do it is this technique.

You tie in a herl by its butt at the bend of the hook. Then you dub with Antron yarn, make a dubbing loop, put the peacock herl in the loop and twist; then you have the shimmering aura around the peacock from the sparkle yarn. The scuba divers I work with say that trout will take this nymph over naturals every time even if both are available to them.

After the dubbing is on, then I put on the bead head.

Q: You don't put the bead head on first, before you dub the body?
LaFontaine: The whole purpose of the bead is to add weight, so here's an optional way to put a bead on a fly. Sometimes you want to use the biggest bead you can, but the problem with that is that it will slip right over the eye of the hook if you put it on the normal way. *[Interviewer's note: Here Gary ties two inch-long pieces of strong tinsel at the head of the fly, slips the tinsel through the eye of the bead, slides the bead onto the fly from the front so the tinsel tie-down is in front of the bead, brings the tinsel pieces back over the bead and ties down the tinsel behind the bead.]* Now you have a bead that's about twice as heavy as the bead that you could slide on the usual way, over the point of the hook. And the whole purpose of the bead is to add weight.

When I'm sitting here devising these flies it's not just to do things differently. I design flies strictly for the reason I want to achieve a particular effect. So here you saw the bead was one effect, and the twist on touch-dubbing was another.

The key for the Twist-Nymph was the problem of how can we combine these two great, proven, magic materials—peacock herl and sparkle yarn.

This is probably one of the best searching nymphs I've ever seen. If I were guiding I'd sure want my clients to use them. You can tie them down to size 18 or so and underwater they have a shimmer, like the bubbles around the gills of a mayfly. It's the added shimmer of the sparkle yarn.

Q: *How much do the split tails add to the pattern?*
LaFontaine: Not much. It's a minor part. Obviously split tails help with certain dry flies but here it's not a big deal.

Q: *And these black beads are brass?*
LaFontaine: Yes, and remember that the ordinary brass bead is about one and a half times heavier than the lead you could wrap around the shank of the fly, so with these big beads it's probably twice as heavy as the lead. It'll go down like a little depth bomb.

Q: *And you use this without any extra weight?*
LaFontaine: That's right. You don't need any additional weight.

Natural Drift Stonefly Nymph

Q: *Well, in addition to that dynamite pattern, what else do you have in your nymph repertoire?*
LaFontaine: For the Western fisherman, I like the Natural Drift Stonefly Nymph. It's one of the first flies I developed. I started watching stoneflies and saw that they don't flip, they don't flop, they don't do somersaults—they pretty much arch their backs and drift in a sort of head-up position. So we designed one with weight in the abdomen and deer hair in the thorax.

Now, for fishing this fly. Bear in mind, that the naturals are migrating toward the banks. All stoneflies, including salmonflies, will migrate in like that. Remember what I said about saying taking ten minutes to sit there before tromping into the stream and stepping on the heads of these fish? Well, if fishermen will get there early, in the early morning hours, and fish this Natural Drift Stonefly Nymph right in tight to the bank, that's where the insects are migrating into, and that's where the trout are following them. It's just a super fly that I wouldn't want to be without in the West.

Q: *Any particular colors?*
LaFontaine: Oh, surprisingly yes. You obviously have your normal colors like black and brown and whatever, but real light cream is a good color. It looks like a molting insect when they shed their skin. They look soft and gray and kind of puttyish.

Q: And is that fly in Trout Flies?

LaFontaine: Yes, they're all in *Trout Flies*. Let me look through here and see what other nymphs I wouldn't want to be without.

There are specific nymphs which you're going to want for specific situations. Like the Deep Sparkle Nymph, which is the corollary of the Emergent Sparkle Pupa. But it's meant to be fished deep. I'd certainly want that.

I think that would be it for starters. But obviously, fishermen should be bringing with them the great patterns like the Hare's Ear, the Pheasant Tail and such.

Q: Do you use those?

LaFontaine: Oh, of course. When I say I carry a lot of flies, it's not just my own flies. I like to use everything. And people will send me flies. I love to experiment with flies.

New Zealand

Q: Have you brought any fly pattern ideas back from New Zealand?

LaFontaine: Not really. From what I've seen of the flies they use I haven't been super impressed by them.

Q: You mean for use up here, or for use down there as well?

LaFontaine: For use anywhere. When we're there we'll test our flies against theirs and outfish the locals because of our flies. Ours are just better flies. The New Zealanders are very much stuck in the English mold. Their feeling is that they don't need a lot of patterns because their streams aren't real rich and so the fish aren't going to be keying on any particular type of insect. It's presentation. But my feeling, like with the Bead Head Twist Nymph, is that you're better off if you can have something that will really pull the fish.

Streamers

Q: What about streamers and soft hackles? Do you use those as well?

LaFontaine: Sure, I use everything. A Woolly Bugger, for instance, is a great fly.

Q: What colors do you prefer in that around here?

LaFontaine: Woolly Bugger? Any shade of black.

Q: Like Henry Ford's automobiles, right? Any other colors for Buggers?

LaFontaine: Probably the best color is burnt orange. That makes a tough crawfish. And trout just love crawdads. Especially big ones. The Missouri is loaded with crawfish, and so is the Jefferson. There are a lot of them in a lot of our rivers. If there is one underutilized food form in fly fishing it's the craw-fish. And a drifted burnt orange Woolly Bugger looks like a crawdad.

Q: What other streamers do you use in these parts?
LaFontaine: I certainly use a full range of them. Like a Hare Sucker for bouncing bottom. For some reason we imitate the sculpin a lot, but trout feed more on suckers than they do on sculpins.

Q: This is the first time I've heard of that pattern. What is it?
LaFontaine: It's a very specific fly for in the spring, after the suckers have spawned and the young suckers are out there. Then the trout will really concentrate on them and I wouldn't want to be without that fly.

Another is the Stub Winged Bucktail. Again, in the book *Trout Flies*. And I'm not trying to pick out all of my flies and say, "God, you've got to have them all." These are ones that if I were coming West I would say, "What do I want to have for sure?" These would be those patterns.

That doesn't mean these are the only ways to skin the cat; they're not. There are a lot of great patterns and a lot of ways of fooling fish. But you've got to fish what you've got confidence in, and these are the ones that I have confidence in. If I didn't have them, I'd feel kind of lost.

Soft-Hackles

Q: What about soft-hackles?
LaFontaine: I'll use soft-hackles and swing them, but I don't use them a tremendous amount. I use them when fish are rising sporadically, when you can't cover any one fish because you can't tell when he's going to come back up. Whereas if you swing a soft-hackle through, it covers so much water that you'll find fish. So I use it as a finder.

Q: Any particular color or pattern?
LaFontaine: The soft-hackles I use are more like the real classic ones. The Partridge and Orange is probably my favorite. With orange floss and only one wrap of partridge, so it's not overdressed.

Clear Wing Spinner

Q: Are there any patterns we've missed, ones that at the end of the season you'd have probably used?
LaFontaine: I use them all. All the flies in these boxes and probably hundreds of others, too. I will mention one dry fly, though, if we can go back to that.

We have great spinner falls out here. I've had people come out with flies from other areas that are hackle flies or Krystal Flash wing spinners and they

23

say, "I can't see 'em!" I started thinking about that, and decided it's because we have so much glare on our water. So I use a Clear Wing Spinner which, even in size 18 or 20, you can see from 30 feet away. And that's a tremendous advantage, because if you can't see a fly you can't fish it. You can't get a good drag-free drift and you can't see where it's covering.

Q: And why can you see this fly so well?
LaFontaine: Well, because of the clear Antron for the wing. It's just like a little beacon out there. And yet that's exactly what the mayfly spinner wing looks like. It's pleated, it gathers air bubbles underneath and it has brightness to it. So it's a great imitation, but again the real advantage is that you can see it. So I'd say that if you're coming out here bring along Clear Wing Spinners.

Q: What Antron material do you use in the wings?
LaFontaine: Clear Antron. Not white, but clear. It comes in various names. You can get some called Hi-Viz.

Personal Fishing Techniques

Q: Moving from flies to techniques, do you have any personal fishing techniques that differ from those of other good fishermen?
LaFontaine: How about starting with techniques for lakes. If there's one untouched paradise out here it's the lakes. You can fish the Madison all year and not get a five-pounder, but I could take you out to any number of lakes and you could fish hard for a week and you'd probably get a five-pounder. So I love lakes.

We've developed a technique. Your running line has to be a monofilament. Can't be a floating running line. Then, for a shooting head you use Hi-D sinking line, about 20 feet of it. Probably an eight-weight. Then you use an eight- or nine-foot leader and a *floating* fly. I like a floating damsel fly, which has foam under the dubbing and is really unsinkable. It's in *Trout Flies*. You use this technique not in deep water, but in water maybe only six to ten feet deep. I won't fish more than ten feet deep. I generally use a lead-core with this rig, and it just sinks like a rock. Goes right down to the bottom, in the weeds. And the fly is trying to float, so every time you twitch it you get a down-up movement that just drives fish crazy.

A couple of years ago I gave a talk to a bass club in Connecticut. I love to fish for bass. While I was there I went fishing with some of the club members. I'd told them about this technique, and they said it would probably work but it wouldn't be as good as plastic worms. Well, we went out fishing and they were real surprised. Of course I wasn't using a damsel fly, I was using a floating minnow. From the same boat, with them using plastic worms, my technique outfished theirs about six to one.

24

I tell that story to bass clubs and ask them why they think that technique works so well. They give all sorts of reasons, but they never get the real reason. The real reason is that the Hi-D, lead-core line goes Bam, right down to the weeds, give a strip, Boom. Give a strip, Boom. That line does something that no spinning lure line can do. That fly line is kicking up the weeds, kicking up the insects and spooking out the minnows and it's a 20-foot chum line coming through the weeds. You all of a sudden have this long, thin chum line with the insects going around, the minnows feeding on them and then the fly comes right through the middle of it and the bass are coming in to feed on the minnows.

Q: You're shuffling!
LaFontaine: It is the deadliest method you can possibly imagine. And it works for trout, too. You can use it from the bank, a float tube or a boat. Wherever you know there's a shallow weed bed.

Q: You mentioned a damsel fly, but what other kind of fly would you use with that?
LaFontaine: Crayfish. Floating crayfish.

Fishing Scummy Backwaters

Q: What other techniques?
LaFontaine: Let's talk about streams. Probably the one different technique I use when guiding is when you come into these scummy backwaters. Like on the Big Hole or the Missouri. Big backwaters, with the grass churning around. A dry fly coming through there will hook onto a piece of grass or drag almost immediately. And the guides are not taking full advantage of these, which are probably the hottest spots in the river, as they go by in a boat. So the technique which we developed is to come up with a pattern called a Slider.

The Slider has a deer hair head with goop on it, that looks like the carapace on a triceratops dinosaur, and when you pull on it, it slides, just skates across the water. So you pound that fly back into the back end of the backwater and start stripping it across and because the fly is skating it's hopping over the little pieces of grass. It's a very specific fly for a very specific situation. So we get to utilize water that nobody else touches, and as far as I'm concerned that's the key to guiding.

Q: Is the Slider in Trout Flies?
LaFontaine: Yes it is. If I can find four or five fish for a client that no one else has even tried to catch, then I've done my job.

Q: Are those generally browns in those backwater places?

LaFontaine: Browns and rainbows. Really. They're really great pieces of water.

Nymphing Techniques

Q: Any other techniques?

LaFontaine: In nymph fishing there are a couple of things that I do. One, to help detect strikes, is use two strike indicators and use fluorescent orange monofilament for the first butt section. The two indicators give you depth perception, and the colored butt section lets you see it curl down into the water. Those things help a lot in sensing takes by the fish, especially the more subtle takes.

The other thing we teach people is to set the hook differently when they're nymph fishing. When you strike underwater you've got to move that fly twice as far and twice as fast, and the way we do that is with what we call the "accordion strike."

The accordion strike is like a single haul. You haul with the line hand while you're lifting the rod with the other hand, so it's like opening up an accordion. Boom. You've doubled the speed and you've doubled the distance. And you've got to realize that it's not like a strike on a dry fly where you see it. With a nymph, by the time you see any indication, no matter how good you are, that fish has had that fly in his mouth for a certain amount of time. He's either spit it out or he's about to spit it out, so you *can't* strike too fast on a nymph.

Q: That's the same way you strike with a bass, pulling with the line hand. It's the opposite of a slip strike, isn't it?

LaFontaine: Exactly. When you go bass fishing you've got to strike hard. When I go bass fishing the first time after a layoff I can't get myself to set the hook, and I lose fish. No matter how much I know, and no matter how hard I try, I can't set the hook. And it's the same thing after a couple of weeks of bass fishing. I go trout fishing and bust off the first five strikes.

Splurging on Equipment

Q: If somebody is going to splurge on a particular piece of equipment what should that be?

LaFontaine: Gore-Tex waders.

Q: You blindsided me. I thought you'd probably say a good rod. Why do you say Gore-Tex waders?

LaFontaine: If there's one problem people have out here it's being comfortable. Often you can't wear neoprene and a lot of the lightweights get cut up by

26

the beaver shoots and stuff like that. I think Gore-Tex waders are great. You're not hot and you don't have all that condensation. I like to be comfortable when I fish. You don't need Gore-Tex in Connecticut but you do out here. You can walk all day long in August with no trees and no shade. They're a godsend. Comfort first Paul, then I'll worry about the fish.

Gary's Reading

Q: What fly fishing publications do you read these days?
LaFontaine: Everything. Magazines and books. Everything that's written. I try to stay current.

Q: If you were to recommend one book, what would it be?
LaFontaine: *Larger Trout for the Western Fly Fisherman* by Charlie Brooks. There's probably no better book for the outsider, someone who has not fished the West. It's still in print, through The Lyons Press. It not only describes specific techniques but gives you the philosophy that you need to conquer the West.

I suppose that if you're coming out here, you should get the guide books. You should study the books on the specific rivers you'll be fishing.

The Future of Fishing

Q: Taking a longer view than techniques, tell me about your views on the future of fishing.
LaFontaine: The problem with our Western rivers, the popular ones, is crowds. They're really getting pounded.

The one thing that infuriates me is people catching so many fish, even with catch and release. I saw an ad the other day in *Fly Fisherman* magazine for the South Fork of the Snake: "Our client caught and released 136 fish." All the studies show that no matter how carefully you release fish, you have about four percent mortality rate. That clown that caught and released 136 fish killed more trout than the bait fisherman who takes his five fish and goes home.

We have to limit the fishing not only to catch and release, but also how many we're catching and releasing. The idea of going for some incredible number of fish a day, making that our goal, is the real problem. I think we have to limit even our catch-and-release pressure on the streams.

Q: Would you try to do that by regulation?
LaFontaine: No. You'd just have to do it as a matter of fishing ethics. Like saying after catching 20 fish could you sit down and smell the roses or something? Look at Sphinx Mountain on the Madison, or just sit down and enjoy the experience?

27

And crowds are a problem. I don't know what we're going to do about it. Do you limit the number of people that can fish the Madison?

Q: How do you view our environmental problems?
LaFontaine: The problem is that at some point sportsmen are going to have to come together. It galls me when a fly fisherman votes for somebody who's bad on environmental issues. Maybe because his views on taxes are good for that voter. But at some point you're going to have to vote against your own self-interest. You're going to need to vote against some other single issues that you may feel very strongly about.

But we have to come together as a unified voice to say: The environment is critical. If we destroy that there is no economics, there is no quality of life, there is no family unit. We're all going to be living in a hellhole. And we've not yet come together that strongly to send that message. So, as a result, the environment is being ignored because legislators know that the voters consider other issues more important. I just think that at some point we're going to have to show some real unity. Not only fly fishermen, but every other type of out-door sport.

Q: What specific environmental issues are most important?
LaFontaine: To start with, there's the proper conduct of mining and lumbering. We need metals and we need wood, but it's a matter of proper practices to produce them. But there's really only one environmental issue, and that's population growth. I don't care how well you do it, how sane your laws are, if the population keeps growing we're going to keep on displacing animals and putting pressure on the water and the land. We need to limit our population growth—and we really need to actually lessen the total population by lowering the birth rate—if we're to preserve the things that are really important.

Craig Mathews

Where to reach him:

Blue Ribbon Fly Shop

315 Canyon Street

West Yellowstone, Montana 59758

Phone: 406/646-7642

Guides professionally now: Yes, on a limited basis. "I don't guide every day now, but I do still guide."

Homewaters: Madison River and Yellowstone Park waters

Born: 1949, Grand Rapids, Michigan

Guiding history: Started guiding in 1979 in West Yellowstone, Montana

Present fishing business affiliation: Partner: Blue Ribbon Fly Shop, West Yellowstone, Montana, and Blue Ribbon Fly Shop on the Madison River, Cameron, Montana; Co-Owner: Yellowstone Park Company, West Yellowstone, Montana.

Publications:

Author: (with John Juracek) *Fly Patterns of Yellowstone*, Blue Ribbon Flies (1987);

Fishing Yellowstone Hatches, Blue Ribbon Flies (1992); (with Clayton Molinero)

The Yellowstone Fly-Fishing Guide, The Lyons Press (1997);

Western Fly Tying Strategies, scheduled for 1998 publication by The Lyons Press;

Numerous articles published in *Fly Fisherman, Fly Rod & Reel, Fly Tyer.*

Craig Mathews and I met to talk fishing on a snowy April morning in West Yellowstone, Montana. We conducted the interview in a basement office room below Craig's shop, Blue Ribbon Flies. Our appointment was for 9:00 a.m., and when I entered the shop there were three tying tables in operation, Craig manning one of them.

Craig is a very personable guy. As we chatted for the recording machine, it was quickly apparent that his people-handling skills were well developed, a useful trait for both his present and former professions, the latter being Chief of Police of West Yellowstone.

Even though we were at his place of business on a working day, Craig permitted but a few brief interruptions of our interview. Throughout our session, he was relaxed, in a feet-on-the-desk sort of way, but nonetheless his manner was poised and businesslike and his answers were articulate and succinct. He has the manner of a person who takes pride in what he's accomplished, yet— having an agenda for his life—knows he has many things yet to do.

Question: *How did you get into guiding, Craig?*
Mathews: I came here from Michigan as a policeman and then ended up as Chief of Police of West Yellowstone when the old chief left. Pretty soon we had a police department with four cops. All of us had at least a bachelor's degree in law enforcement. Nobody made over 10,000 bucks, but we all fished and had a great time. We ran the cop shop.

In 1979 Gregg Lilly asked me if I'd consider doing some guiding. I agreed to guide a day or two a week, and to make a long story short, a year later we opened this shop. Of course, since then I've done a lot of guiding in this area.

Clients Who Ask and Listen
Q: Based on what you've observed, how can folks get the most out of a guided fishing experience?
Mathews: The first thing I love to have people do is just come in and listen. Tell the guide what they expect, but then let the guide tell them the best options. Have some patience with the guide, and ask him questions.

I don't know what it is, but people are often embarrassed to ask questions or ask for help. They will accept help or suggestions, but they seem to be afraid to ask for it. Like help with their casting. Or maybe in some cases they think they're a whole lot better than they are. And there's a certain macho thing there sometimes, I think.

An experienced guide has a tremendous wealth of knowledge. People should ask a lot of questions and tap that knowledge, try to bleed him of that knowledge.

30

Q: Is that the kind of client you like to guide, one that asks a lot of questions?
Mathews: Yes, I like to see a guy that comes in here and is all ears. So often they come in with the idea that they just want to catch big fish. But most of the people like that, if you sit them down, put a cup of coffee in front of them and ease them into the day, usually you can bring them around to appreciating other aspects of the fishing experience. It may take a day or two of mellowing out to really do the job, because many of them are in really high stress jobs.

Every now and then we have clients who come in and the first thing they have to do is get on the phone and call their office. And that kind of bugs me. We've even gone so far as to tie up all the phone lines when we know a client is going to do that in the morning. Sometimes they don't get out the door all day.

They get on a mission, there's some buyout and all this happy crap they're working on, and pretty soon there they sit, just being a nervous wreck the whole day. I've even told secretaries that their boss isn't going to be in today, that he's on the Beaverhead, when in fact I know he's in the store when I'm talking to her.

These guys need some time away from their work, and some of these secretaries drive 'em completely insane. Which is too bad. Here's a guy out here trying to enjoy himself and we'll get faxes here just laying all over the place. "Call me right away, and blah, blah, blah," and you think, "That poor son-of-a-gun."

And a lot of times I don't tell them about a fax until they come back in from fishing. They'll tell me I'm doing them a favor, and I've never had one get upset.

More To Fishing Than Fishing

Q: In an earlier answer, you mentioned pointing out to people some "other aspects of the fishing experience." What other aspects did you mean?
Mathews: I mean things like being in a wild setting, seeing the beauty of this area, learning about its history and appreciating the wildlife and everything that goes along with fishing out here. People tend to be more in tune with that now.

Several times a year I'll have people go out with a guide and when they come in I'll say, "How was your day?" They'll say, "This was a great day. And we never even fished."

I'll say, "What?" And the response is something like, "Well, we wanted to look at the Earthquake Visitors Center, and then we asked the guide about the Native Americans that inhabited this part of the world and we looked at tepee rings."

"And you didn't fish?"

"No, but we had a wonderful day. And it was by our choice that we didn't fish. We started asking him about the flora and fauna, the this and the that, and pretty soon we'd spent the whole day looking and never fishing."

Usually that happens with a husband and wife, and maybe a kid along.

Q: What do you like best about the guiding experience? How does it compare with your prior occupations?

Mathews: I enjoy the people. At least in this area, there are so many interesting folks that come through. From all walks of life. I've never met a client I didn't like. Everybody has his quirks, but if you can give people a real nice experience on the river, that's what it's all about.

And let's face it. Fly fishermen usually don't argue with you, and you don't have to put 'em in handcuffs, unlike like my previous profession.

The Joy of Beginners

Q: Back when you were actively guiding did you mind guiding someone with no skills at all, like a husband and wife showing up and she's never held a fly rod before?

Mathews: Seems like invariably she would outfish him. Raw beginners always have a great time, especially women, and they usually outfish the old man. Most guides would rather deal with raw beginners than with a guy who fishes once a year and has developed a lot of bad habits.

One thing about beginners is that they appreciate the fish they catch. Get them a fish of any size and they're in heaven.

Tackle Buying Mistakes

Q: In your experience, what mistakes do people commonly make in buying tackle and equipment?

Mathews: One thing is that people often buy flies in their hometowns and their flies don't work here. That's OK from our standpoint, because we do sell flies that do work here. But, from the client's standpoint, he will have to buy his flies twice.

Another thing, some people show up with boots or waders without felt soles, and that can cause a lot of wet clothes.

Q: Do people often pay too much or too little for tackle? Like buying stuff more expensive than required, or too cheap to get the job done?

Mathews: I think the biggest mistake people make is that they buy a beginner's outfit. Then they quickly outgrow it, and are kicking themselves because they didn't get the best. I see it all the time. I often tell people, "You're going to come back to me later and buy the best, so you might as well do it now."

I think where anglers really scrimp is on fly lines. They keep them too long. If someone's fishing 20 or 30 days a year, he should buy a new fly line every year. Same way with tippets. They'll save them from year to year, even 4X, 5X and 6X. I tell them, "Throw 'em away, buy new ones." If they don't buy new tippets they'll spend more money on flies that break off than they would have spent on tippet. Those tippets do go bad just sitting there.

Fishermen are funny; they'll spend a lot of money on a rod and reel, then they'll scrimp on line and tippet.

Expensive Reels

Q: Is an expensive reel something you'd recommend?
Mathews: Around here, forget it. Drag is not that important. Every now and then you hook the fish of a lifetime, and you're going, "Dang it, I wish I had a better drag." But that's pretty unusual.

We talk people out of buying Abels because, we tell them, you can buy two Orvis CFO's for that money. In other words, for this kind of fishing, an expensive drag is not that big of a deal.

Q: Switching from equipment to fishing techniques, what common mistakes does the average fisherman make?
Mathews: They fish in the wrong places, for one thing. Most people aren't used to a big river like the Madison, and they tend to fish it by walking right up the middle of it where the trout aren't but where the whitefish are. You point out to them that they want to fish the edges, the margins, that's where the fish are. Fish it as you would a small stream, don't pay any attention to what's going on out in the middle.

Cast Less Line

Q: How about casting mistakes?
Mathews: In casting, everybody's into distance. You'll put a guy into rising fish, maybe ten feet away, and he's got 50 feet of line out, casting beyond those rising fish, and you wonder what the heck's going on here. Then you've got to regroup and say, "You see all those heads out there? Those are trout. Let's try to throw real short casts, maybe take just one mend, and you'll get those fish." So many times that sort of thing happens.

For me, personally, on the Madison and the streams around here, an average cast is 15 or 20 feet. And that's the distance from where my feet are to where the fly lands. Sometimes I'm only casting leader, or just the tippet.

And I've had the experience in guiding from a drift boat, of rowing so as to get a guy close in to the bank—where the fish are—and he's firing it all the way across the river. Not only are the fish not there, he has so much line out that he couldn't hook a fish if he had to. Most people tend to fish too long a line out here. Rather than work to get into a good position they throw a 50-foot cast when they should throw a ten-foot cast.

Importance of Good Position

Q: What do you teach people about casting from a good position?

Mathews: Position is a very big thing with me. I teach people that if a fish rises they should study the situation a little bit instead of just jumping in and flailing the water from wherever they happen to be standing.

So often I've seen anglers be fishing and when they see a fish rise—I don't care where they're at or how far from the rise—they start casting to that fish.

Q: What would you do if you saw a rise?

Mathews: I'll let that fish rise four or five times. I like for him to establish a little confidence in what he's feeding on. It also gets me a little confident too because I can usually get into a position where I want to be. I may want to be a little bit above him or below him. But I want to give myself time to see his riseform, to figure out what he may be feeding on.

I just don't want to throw a fly out there and hope that he's gonna take it. I'd much rather give him a fly that represents what I know he's feeding on than risk putting him down with a fly he isn't going to eat anyway. Or maybe put him down with drag because I'm casting from a bad position.

I spend a lot of time getting close to the fish. I want to see that fish's eye. I like to get real close to 'em. I find that if you spend time you can get right up on 'em. I think then you can see your fly better, you can watch what the fish is taking. I mean if he's taking a brown drake you can't see that a mile away.

The Fisherman As Hunter

Q: In listening to you I sense that you bring a lot of the attitude of the hunter, and hunting skills, into your fishing. Is that correct?

Mathews: That is correct. Often, particularly with trout in skinny water, it's as much hunting as it is fishing. And I think that's what is really intriguing about it.

You can chuck and chance it on a river, but that's just like shooting up into the air hoping a duck will fly into your pattern. I like to find one individual fish feeding. You watch that one fish and you can learn a lot about him. You may see him move differently when he takes a fly. Again, you can see that eye, and you put that cast in there and he comes over. You know exactly what side of the mouth he's going to take your fly with because you've seen how he turns to take naturals. You get to know a little bit about that fish even before you catch him. I like that.

Mending and Line Control

Q: In an earlier answer you mentioned mending line. Do folks generally understand how mending and line control work?

Mathews: I've often had clients who have no idea of what mending is, or of taking in the slack. They'll throw an upstream cast and pretty soon they've got this huge belly of line and the fly's going a hundred miles an hour beyond their line and they're looking for their fly. And in drift boats they'll take way too much line off their spool. But I think that things are getting a whole lot better as clients seem to be learning more about line control.

Q: Are there any other common mistakes that folks make?

Mathews: It always amazes me how many people can't see their fly. They, for instance, cast their fly upstream—maybe even a hopper pattern. They'll be looking upstream, as if watching their fly, but the fly has already passed them by. Or you can yell "strike" if the fish takes it and they don't see anything. I'm really surprised at how few people can see their fly or see rising fish until you spend some time with them.

Bringing Fish In Quickly

Q: What do you teach people about landing fish?

Mathews: I teach people to snub 'em up and bring 'em in. I've gotten into discussions with people on stream where they're fighting a 16-inch fish for 10 minutes. I just scream at 'em, "Get that fish in!" With the new tippets that are out there now you can really pour the heat on these fish. You can't break off 4X. I mean you can't break it. And 5X is tough to break.

I tell 'em to give the fish a jump and a run then just bring him on in, because you're gonna kill that fish if you don't get him in and get that hook out of him. So my thing is, after the initial run or two just crank 'em right in. And they come in. They do. You bet they do.

As for how to hold the rod when playing a fish, I do a lot of holding my rod parallel to the water and switching the rod from the right side to the left side. That turns their head and you tend to be able to bring 'em right in. I've had very good luck with that.

Preferred Fly Patterns

Q: I know that you and your shop take pride in the flies you turn out. What are the patterns that you like to use around here?

Mathews: Our Sparkle Dun, as a mayfly imitation, is one. We tie that in various sizes and colors for the various hatches around here. I use very few hackle flies any more. Not even Parachutes. The Parachutes work fine but the sparkle duns are easier to tie and they work better, too.

I never use an Elk Hair Caddis any more. I use a fly that we've come up with called an X-caddis. Like what a Sparkle Dun is for a mayfly, this X-caddis is for caddis. It has a trailing shuck, a dubbed body and a deer hair wing. And for a caddis dry fly, that's all I use. If they're taking emergers, I trim the wing off and with that trailing Z-lon shuck they take it for an emerger. Or I just pull it under and let it pop up in front of them.

I'll use a soft-hackle because it's fun to tie. Also they're pretty and they work.

I use very few patterns, unlike some of my friends who have so many patterns they don't know where half their flies are.

Dries vs. Subsurface Flies

Q: In your personal fishing do you have any preferences between dries and subsurface flies?

Mathews: Not really. It all depends on what the fish are feeding on. To me, the fly you fish with depends on what the fish are taking. For instance, if a fish is nymphing, I'd rather catch that fish on a nymph than have him come up to a big dry fly that may just attract him to take it.

So often you see fish feeding on the Madison and you think they're taking dry flies. No way. They're taking nymphs, right in the surface. You can throw dry flies at those big browns all day long, and you may get a little rainbow that swims over and takes your fly. But as soon as you put on a *Baetis* nymph, those feeding fish will take that nymph. That to me is what it's all about. Finding the bigger fish and taking them on their terms on what they're eating.

Fly Sizes

Q: How about sizes of flies that you use?

Mathews: I use a lot of tiny flies to imitate the tiny naturals, even on the big water. I mean #20s and #22s. We often get midge emergences on the Madison. People miss the boat there. They'll see a fish feeding and they won't see anything on the water, so immediately they'll put on a #10 Royal Wulff. And hope.

They never consider trying to throw an individual midge pupa or a #22 adult midge at that fish. But that's what he's feeding on, and you're going to catch far more fish if you're using what he's feeding on. So I tend to use much smaller flies than most people will even consider.

It depends on the hatch, but with Blue-Winged Olives I fish #24s all the time. The naturals may look bigger than that on the water, unless you really look at them carefully. I don't have a problem using flies that small, but some people do.

I think a small fly hooks a fish better than a larger fly. You put a #24 in a fish and you can't get that fly out half the time. That thing buries in there and really holds better than, say, a #16. There's less leverage to work it out. In fact, you'd better make sure those small flies are barbless or you're in real trouble getting them out.

Uncommon Tying Materials

Q: In your shop do you use any offbeat materials in tying, any materials that aren't commonly used?

Mathews: I don't know if we can call them 'not-commonly used' any longer because it seems like whatever we come out with, Orvis and L.L. Bean will have it next year. For instance, Z-lon. We and John Betts popularized Z-lon. We use it in our Serendipities, trailing shucks and wings and those sorts of things. A few years ago somebody would have said, "Boy, is that material off the wall," but now everybody uses it.

Also we use sharptail grouse and sage hen feathers. No one considered using those birds a few years ago. Sharptail grouse is a beautiful golden plover substitute, and you can't get golden plover anymore. So we've made those materials available to fly tiers. And I see them appearing in other catalogues.

And in tying soft hackles, for instance, we still use Hungarian partridge, but we also use sage hen, blue grouse and quail.

Long Leaders, Light Tippets and Double-Taper Lines

Q: What do you prefer as to tippets and leaders?

Mathews: I'll use from three feet to six feet of tippet. The shortest dry-fly leader I use will be 16 feet, sometimes 20 feet. It depends on where I'm fishing. I think that's another problem people have: they're afraid to fish small tippets. You say 6X or three-pound, and they say, "Oh my God! I can't use that." I fish a lot of 6X and my standard is that I won't, as a rule, go any heavier than 5X. I hate to go smaller than 6X, but I'll fish 7X when I need to.

The purpose of the long tippet, incidentally, is to get a longer drag-free float than some people might think you need. I'm a big believer in that, especially on the Firehole and on spring creeks, so I'll throw pile-casts where you get a whole bunch of tippet at the end, and the tippet can take its time before it finally straightens out. You have so many little currents in the Firehole and spring creeks. You need to bear in mind that the tippet serves a function not only because it's less visible than the rest of the leader, but also it behaves differently in the water than the rest of the leader. It doesn't affect the drifting action of the fly as much as a heavier leader material would.

Q: Do you have any strong preferences as to types of fly line?

Mathews: I use a lot of double-taper lines. I very seldom use a weight-forward line. That's because I think you can make a lot better presentation with the double-taper and I think they go through the wind better than weight-forward. I know that's not conventional wisdom.

People say that you can "punch right through with weight-forward," They think that they can get through wind with a heavier line, but for me a finer diameter rod and finer diameter line cuts the wind easier than a big, heavy rod and line. People try to gun lines too much, anyway. It's not muscle that cuts the wind, it's that fly line going psheww!

I should mention that in fishing shorter distances, wind is less of a factor. And of course there are some days so windy that I don't care what you're using, you're not going to get that fly out there.

Rod Preferences

Q: You like to cast short distances and use light tippets. What rod do you prefer?

Mathews: I like a real soft rod, like a Winston traditional graphite, 9 foot, 4 weight as a rule.

As for the real light rods, like one and two weight, there's a place for them, too. No wind, small flies. But I have trouble landing a good size fish with the darned things sometimes. You need something to get him in with. I don't want to mess with a fish too long. I want to get him in and get him released. He's a lot better off for it and so am I.

Humor On the Stream

Q: While you were out there guiding did funny stuff ever happen?

Mathews: Well, one time Nick Lyons hooked his wife on a backcast and she took off running. I've got a picture of it.

Another time a fellow named Bill Cass and his wife were fishing with me and she hooked a dog, a husky it was. And that was pretty funny. Then a couple of times I've had people hook those terns down on the Henry's Fork.

One that I remember real well was when I was fishing with Paul Studebaker a couple of years ago. He had about $700 in a new Sage rod and a CFO reel. We went to the Firehole and he's so excited to be there he starts fishing from the bank without even putting his waders on. It's snowing and the fish are rising. He catches a couple and then he breaks off. So he lays his rod down on a piece of sagebrush and starts to suit-up with his waders and other equipment. Then here comes a bull elk. The bull elk sees the rod, goes over to the rod and gets the line tangled with his rack. Paul starts yelling at the bull elk, and that only caused the bull elk to start running. And as it ran the rod was slapping him on the hind end, so the faster he ran the more he got slapped. He crossed the river, went up in the hills and Paul's new rod and reel were gone forever.

One of my favorites though happened when I was fishing with Bob Hoar. We were wade fishing and we saw a guy on the other side of the stream with a creel. It was obvious from the wetness on the canvas creel that it wasn't empty. Bob just came unglued. He goes over there and he's reading that guy the frickin' riot act. Finally the guy says, "Sir," he says, "I'm picking up empty beer cans from the bottom of the creek."

Q: Does anything happen out there that upsets you?
Mathews: It upsets me when people kill fish in a catch-and-release area. That really upsets me.

Also, I get pretty upset when anglers wade through spawning beds. I know it's just ignorance on their part, but it angers me. I've found that if you go up and tell them what they're doing—wiping out 90 percent of the nest by wading through it—they're happy to comply. They just didn't know what they were doing.

We've been after the state to shut down the Madison in the spring to give the rainbows a chance to spawn. I believe that a lot of the decline in the rainbow population on the Madison is probably due to increased angling pressure and people destroying the nests.

Limiting Fishing

Q: Speaking of such things, do you have any suggestions for improvements in fish and river management?
Mathews: Well, for one thing, the Madison doesn't need any more guides on it. In our shop we decided some years ago to limit the number of our guides and we don't add any new ones unless another guide dies or retires.

And I believe that we're going to have to limit the number of fishermen, as well. My idea is that if you get a fishing license ending in an odd number, then you only fish on odd numbered days of the month, and if it ends in an even number then you fish even numbered days.

I can see where we're heading toward something like that on certain rivers, anyway. At least I'd like to see that. We have too many fly fishermen on some of our rivers. That's wonderful, but it ain't so wonderful.

Johnny Gomez

Where to reach him:

Abe's Fly Shop

Navajo Dam, New Mexico 87419

Phone: 505/632-2194

Professionally guides now: Yes

Homewaters: San Juan River

Born: 1961, Gallup, New Mexico

Where grew up: Four Corners area

Guiding history: Has guided year-round on the San Juan since 1990.

Present fishing business affiliations: Abe's Fly Shop, as guide, fly designer and tier. Wife, Gina, ties flies for Abe's as well.

I sought out Johnny Gomez for an interview because another respected San Juan River guide characterized him as "The Guru of San Juan Guides."

He is lean, wiry and full of energy. It doesn't take long to sense the questing of an active mind looking for new answers to old questions, and even coming up with a few new questions to boot. It's quite apparent that Johnny's life is largely the river and its fish.

Johnny guides an impressive 300+ guiding days per year on the San Juan. That's close to three times the number of days that many hard-working Montana guides get to ply their trade. He commutes for work on the river from his home in Farmington, about 30 miles distant. Our interview was taped at the dining room table of Johnny's house. The place is new and modern, and clean in a way that bespeaks of a woman's supervision of the housekeeping.

Toward the end of our session Johnny's wife, Gina, returned home from errands. She, according to Johnny, is the real fly tier of the family, and he asked her if she'd mind tying up some fast samples of the tiny San Juan flies he'd been telling me about. She smilingly complied, tying up a small handful of 22s and 24s.

While she tied, Johnny and I took a break to look over some color snapshots of his clients with San Juan trout. Included were some shots of fish in the 10-pound range. As to each of those monster trout, Johnny had a detailed description of the catching; every one had come from the still or slow-moving backwater eddies of the river. He said there was a lesson to be learned there.

Question: How long have you been guiding, Johnny?

Gomez: For six years now. All on the San Juan and all as a guide for Abe's [Abe's Fly Shop, Navajo Dam, New Mexico]. I grew up here in the Four Corners area, spent all my life here.

Q: Are you involved in the fishing business in other ways, as well?

Gomez: Well, I tie gobs of flies to sell at Abe's. My wife, Regina, does that too, full time. Gina can really whip them out. We do a lot of glass-bead flies, and actually I introduced those on the San Juan. Like the Green Head Lady and the Cherry Bomb.

Selecting a Guide

Q: When a person decides to take a guided fishing trip, what's the best way to find a good guide?

Gomez: Well in our shop, in Abe's, I know that when somebody comes in and wants a guide they try to match them with a guide that they'll enjoy fishing with. Maybe the person says that they want somebody who has a lot of patience. Or maybe the person wants to learn a lot rather than catch a lot of fish.

Then, not only do they match the person with the right guide, but they'll tell the guide what the person's expectations are so the guide will know what to emphasize and what to expect. They also tell us something about the person's experience. And I think most outfitters are good about doing stuff like that.

Q: What's your favorite kind of client to take fishing?
Gomez: Somebody who'll pay attention, who'll listen. I like people who just want to come out and have a good time, and the size of fish doesn't really matter to them. Somebody who likes to talk and who's open-minded, someone who's willing to try anything. Like not being afraid to fish with an indicator or to throw dries if I suggest it. Those kinds of people listen to the guide, and they let you help them.

Kids make great clients. They're learning, they're focused on it. And people who've never held a fly rod before, whatever age, are real easy to guide because they don't have any bad habits. And I really like it when people have something to add, like flies that they've tied. You learn as much from your clients as you do from any other source.

Q: What common mistakes do people bring along to their guided fishing experience?
Gomez: Slow sets when they're nymphing are a real common mistake. And they don't load their backcasts properly. On dry-fly fishing, they set their hooks too fast.

Another big mistake that people make is not having line control after the hookup. They let the fish get slack and the fish gets off.

Slow Down and Take It Easy
Q: If you could give people a few rules to follow to help them in their non-guided fishing, what would some of those rules be?
Gomez: First, slow down. People get in too much of a hurry. When I'm out guiding I see a lot of people on their own, and I always notice that they seldom seem to stop, take a look around and see just where the fish might be sitting. They'll just charge right out into the water, maybe spooking fish that were right up next to the bank.

When I'm guiding I try to get people to calm down and take it easy. If they don't they get hurried and excited and their adrenaline gets to pumping and when they're in that state they err a lot. They throw a lot of knots in their leader because they're hurrying their casts. They break off when they strike. Another result of hurrying is not letting your fish run. You've got to go out there, take a few deep breaths, look at your water, see where you want to fish, approach calmly and then start your fishing. The best thing to do is to take your time and enjoy it. Don't rush your fishing adventure.

Q: What other tips?

Gomez: If you're new to an area, it's a real good idea to go into a shop and talk to people there, or talk to a guide. Find out what's going on there.

I see a lot of people come in, buy flies and never ask how to fish them. I see it every day. They never talk to anybody to find out what the fish are feeding on, whether to fish shallow or fish deep, do I need light tippet or can I use heavier tippet. If I go somewhere else to fish I'll go in a shop and find those things out.

People will be out on the water fishing the right bugs in the wrong way—maybe not using enough weight, not sweeping it at the end of the drift (which is where a lot of fish take a nymph, especially with the bead patterns) and not fishing the right part of the riffles.

Hire a Guide For the First Day

Q: What other suggestions?

Gomez: One thing I've seen in my years of guiding is that people will fish for five or six days without success, then take a guided trip. After that trip their fishing will be better even if they're fishing without a guide. But they've lost some good fishing by waiting. So that's why, if you're going to get a guide, you should get one the first day, even if it's only for a half day. It'll make a big, big difference in your fishing for the rest of your days on that river. You can learn what patterns are working and also the techniques for that river. I consider using a guide on the first day to be real important.

The best thing to do is to call in advance, tell them what you need and about your experience and what kind of guide you're looking for. Say whether you're looking for an aggressive guide or for a guide who is real calm and takes his time, whether you want to catch a lot of fish or whether you primarily want to learn some new stuff. And definitely do all this ahead of time, about two or three months before your trip.

Landing Fish

Q: Are there techniques that you teach people, like landing fish properly?

Gomez: As to landing fish properly, I try to fish a heavy enough tippet to land fish quickly. You don't want to overfight your fish. I find that in deep water it's better to keep the rod more horizontal rather than up and down. But most of the time I like to hold the rod tip up, vertical to the water surface. Also, I hold the rod back and make them fight against the bend of the rod. It actually works like a spring and makes it harder for them to break the leader. And when I'm pulling his head up, by keeping the rod vertical, then he can't dig his head down and use the current to keep himself in the water. And once his head is out of the water, then he's out of his own control and you can pretty well do with him what you want.

And I'm real aggressive in landing fish too. I don't care if I break some off, especially right in front of me. When my clients are taking a long time landing fish I tell them, "Your fishing is keeping you from fishing." Usually, they'd be happier getting on to the next fish.

Another thing is that people keep their fish out of the water too long. I always tell people to hold their breath, and if you need a breath then the fish needs to go back in the water. And of course, always wet your hands and don't squeeze the fish; let him rest in your palms. One thing I do is talk to the fish a lot [here Johnny demonstrates with a sound like a strangled clucking, the kind of noise a fish might make out of water if it could]. For some reason, I don't know why, that settles them down. I learned that from another guide, Lloyd Rogers.

Q: Do you use a net?

Gomez: Yeah, I use a catch-and-release net, and on our guide trips we use big rubber basket-like nets. Some nets are hard on fish, like knotted nylon, and except for the big rubber ones, catch-and-release nets are best for the fish. The shallowness of the catch-and-release net is good too. That way the fish and flies don't tangle up in it. If you have a deep net and want to make it shallow, just tie a knot in it. If you need a deep net for other fishing, you can take the knot out.

Agitating Nymphs

Q: In your own fishing do you have any fishing techniques that are different from the way most other people go about it?

Gomez: Yes, I guess I do. I agitate nymphs a lot. Instead of going with a dead drift I'll make them move. As you know, the San Juan is a slow -moving river a lot of times, and I think giving the nymphs some action helps the fishing.

I use a loop in the line downstream, pulling the bugs with the current to make them move downstream.

Q: You intentionally interfere with the dead-drift of the nymphs?

Gomez: Fish will hit nymphs on agitation. They don't have to be a complete dead drift. I've learned that sometimes when people throw a bad mend that moves the indicator, then right after that mend there'll be a serious strike. One thing about bugs is they're not motionless. They do swim.

Q: So when someone says that a nymph should be fished drag-free like a dry fly, you'd disagree with that?

Gomez: I'd disagree. I have more success fishing a nymph with a little agita-tion, a little pull on the line, a little drag on the line. You've got to think about it. Look at the sweep. When you get to the end of the drift and you get a big sweep, that's when you get a lot of hits. When you agitate the nymph as it's going down the drift, it's the same thing.

On days when fishing is slow I'll tell my clients to agitate it a little bit. They'll ask me what I mean. I tell them to give me a six-inch pull on the indicator on the downstream side. You get a guy to do that and it brings on strikes.

With beginners in a boat, if they're having trouble agitating the flies, I'll put the brakes on the boat in the current to agitate the flies; it's like putting an end to their drift by using boat speed. That makes the flies act like a sweep at the end of a drift. It works. If I don't pick up any fish on that sweep, then I'll row to catch up with the speed of the flies, and I can sweep several times as I'm going down a drift, giving an emerger look to the fly every time it sweeps up.

Q: Does that mean that if a guy mends and accidentally moves his indicator he doesn't need to feel guilty?
Gomez: Not guilty at all. When clients do that I tell them not to worry about it, to do it more. Sometimes I'll ask for the rod and say, "Watch this." I'll cast out and keep agitating again and again, and Bam!, they'll hit it right away. I mean it looks like you're working a streamer.

A lot of the guides on the San Juan are using agitation on their drifts. You fish a mayfly or a midge emerger with a Woolly Bugger and you get twice the strikes, three times the strikes, you would with just a dead drift. I definitely disagree with using a complete dead drift. I hardly ever fish 100 percent dead drifts any more.

Q: And you fish nymphs how many days a year on the San Juan?
Gomez: About 316 days a year.

Work Structure to Find Fish
Q: What other techniques do you have that are different?
Gomez: One thing I do, and I firmly believe in it, is work structure. Edges and points, for instance. A lot of people will go out and just work a drift in open water.

A lot of times, when there's not a big hatch, I'll come in and work inclines, declines, mounds, edges and in front and in back of little points. I call it an incline when the bottom is coming up, and you can tell that from the surface movement of the water. Of course we know the river so well, being on it all the time, that we pretty well know where the inclines, declines and mounds are.

I find trout hanging around structure almost like the way a bass would, especially in slow water. They'll hold around pockets where the water is actually still, or the water has back-eddied. I find a lot of big fish sitting in pockets, still-water pockets.

Q: Even rainbows, or just browns in that still water?

Gomez: Yes, rainbows. And 90 percent of the big fish that people catch with me on the San Juan are in still water. Just off the current. The current will bring food in, and they'll sit in that still water because they don't have to work.

I'll have my clients cast into the seam and let the current bring it into the still water. And the tendency for a lot of people is to pick it up and cast it again right away, the moment the indicator stops moving. I'll say, "Leave it, leave it, leave it." Booom! They'll take a lot of big fish out of still water, just after the current has pushed into it. And sometimes I have them agitate the rig right through the still water, in six-inch pulls, and definitely get hits. All the time. It's amazing.

One thing about big fish, they're lazy. They don't want to work for their food.

Q: Big fish are lazier than little fish?

Gomez: You betcha. I've had the experience of having other guides working out in the currents, and I'll come back and work just off the current into the still water. They're picking up a lot of little fish, we're hitting big fish. It makes a big difference.

Fish the Banks

Q: What other tricks of the trade do you have?

Gomez: Another thing I have clients do is fish the bank, casting toward the bank. Either wading or from a boat. I have them cast right up to the edge of the water, pull it off the bank toward you and you're pulling it right down that decline. And a lot of fish will hold right against the bank. As I said, trout do hold next to structure.

Fishing the bank is real important. A lot of guys, when they're wade fishing, walk right to the bank and start casting out, but the best thing to do is to start fishing along the bank and then work your way out.

Q: What else?

Gomez: Another thing I'll do is fish pockets.

Q: Pockets? You mean pocket water behind big rocks?

Gomez: No, no, no. Pockets where you're out in open water, and there are dips in the bottom. I mean a bottom that looks like moguls in a ski area. You cast out and you're going to be hitting some bottom with the shot. But don't strike at your little bumps on the indicator; wait for a complete pull-down.

What you're doing is coming across those little pockets, little valleys between the moguls, and that's where your fish will lie. So as your flies come across you're going to hit a little ground then dip into the deep spot between the moguls. So what I'm looking at on the indicator is I'm getting a little twitch, a little twitch, a little twitch, then I'll say, "There!"

Q: Do you have your clients fish more from the boat, or while wading?
Gomez: I do both, but I have a tendency to fish more from the boat because it's easier to fish deep water from a boat, and I find more big fish in deep water.

Preferred Nymphing Setups

Q: Since you do a lot of nymphing, let me ask what kind of setup you use on your nymphing rig. Is your setup fairly conventional?
Gomez: We fish a lot of quick-sight leaders. Those are the ones with a piece of fluorescent orange or chartreuse Amnesia up by the indicator, built right into the butt section. A quick-sight leader is tapered and the color blends into the leader about mid-way down. Both Orvis and Umpqua sell them. One thing about them is that you can see how your drift is working and you can pick up light takes on them. Especially when the fish are suspended and you're using light shot because you want a slow sink. A lot of times when they're suspended like that they'll hit it so light that you won't even see the indicator move; you'll see the line tighten up. That's why the quick-sights are so important.

On the San Juan, what we call an average leader is eight feet from the strike indicator to the shot, and after that you have 16 inches to your fly and another 16 inches to your next fly. If the fishing is slow I'll sometimes only have six inches between the two flies.

Another setup I use I call a Trifecta. Sixteen inches below the shot, instead of a fly, I'll put on a little piece of colored yarn, then sixteen inches below that I'll put on a fly, then six inches from that another fly. The yarn is operating as an attractor.

Q: Sixteen inches is more distance than people usually use between shot and fly. Why do you use the longer length?
Gomez: I think it makes a big difference. It keeps the shot away from your flies. Definitely fish will move over to let things, like a piece of moss, go by. Why shouldn't they move over to let shot go by. There are times that I'm running two feet away from the shot to my first fly.

Using Strike Indicators

Q: Do you ever fish nymphs without a strike indicator?
Gomez: I do, but for the clients it's hard. Especially on the San Juan because in your slower-moving water you definitely will miss a lot of strikes.

Q: Where do you put the strike indicator? What kind of indicator do you prefer?

Gomez: I put the strike indicator right at the fly line. I never vary that. I make my adjustments down below. If I have to shorten up, I'll shorten down below.

I always use a small indicator. I use a poly yarn indicator a little smaller than my thumbnail, and I use black because they're less apt to be attractive to the fish. Fish will look up to color, and I've had them hit yellow or red indicators. I've never had them hit black. They might if there was a big mayfly hatch or midge cluster hatch coming, and you ought to be throwing dries then anyway.

But we do a lot of deepwater nymphing on the San Juan. There are times we have the shot ten feet down from the indicator, and you've got to be at ten feet or you won't get 'em. They get down deep and sometimes you've got to throw a lot of weight.

Q: When you want to nymph shallower what do you do? Lighten weight, shorten the leader or both?

Gomez: You can just go into micro-shot to fish shallower. And you have to adjust your weight as to how fast your water's moving and to where your fish are sitting. Even in deep, slow water fish will suspend to feed. Then you can go with micro-shot or a brass bead. Most of the time when I run a brass-bead fly I'll make it the top fly. I think you get a better drift that way, the lower fly stays up. And most of the time they'll hit your lower fly.

Using Multiple Flies

Q: Where would you put an egg pattern, the upper or lower fly?

Gomez: I always put the egg pattern above, unless I'm fishing a leech. With a leech, I'll fish the egg under it, all the time. We fish the leech a lot because the San Juan has a lot of nematodes in it even though there are no leeches. We use Woolly Buggers and Rabbit Hair Leeches in black, white, brown, orange and olive. We use a lot of orange here.

I also like a Woolly Bugger above for your first fly and then your emergers and mayflies as your bottom flies.

Q: How many nymphs do you ordinarily fish with, and how do you connect them?

Gomez: I usually use two flies, seldom one and seldom three. I tie them right in line, tying right onto the bend of the hook of the first fly. I use lighter tippet between the flies to avoid the loss of both flies if I break off a

48

fish on the bottom fly. Like if the tippet above the first fly is 4X then I'll use 5X for the second fly. And those leader sizes are about as low as we go.

Selecting Tackle

Q: How important is expensive tackle to people who come here to fish?

Gomez: When people ask me what rod they should get to learn with I always tell them to go ahead and buy a good rod. As you advance you're going to get one anyway, and you might as well learn with a good rod. It'll save you money in the long run.

Q: How important is an expensive reel on the San Juan?

Gomez: With a disc you can dial in just the drag you want, fine-tune it. But as long as a reel has a good adjustable drag system you don't have to spend a lot of money on a reel. You can go with a Battenkill; that's a click drag and you can do just fine.

Q: How about other items of equipment?

Gomez: A good double-taper fly line. I say double-taper because they cast nice. And if you're out on the river and fish start to rise, then you can fish dries better with a double-taper.

As for mending, I don't find too much difference between double-taper and weight-forward, but I believe having your line clean and well greased makes a big difference. And always mend with your rod tip up, not down. Basically, when you mend you should try to bring the line off the water as far toward the indicator as you can, then flip right or left. And that's why you keep it greased, to be able to lift it off the water quickly and easily. You should clean your line every time you fish it. I do.

Those Unusual San Juan Patterns

Q: You folks who fish the San Juan have such unusual nymph patterns. Why is it that you don't use patterns like Pheasant Tails and Hare's Ears like we find on most Western waters?

Gomez: Well, the reason I don't fish just your basic Pheasant Tail or your basic Hare's Ear is because I went in a couple of steps further into what I call bi-luminescence.

Bi-luminescence is real important because bugs give off a shine and the edge of having that shine on your flies makes a big difference. One thing too, on the San Juan, we went to imitating the bugs a little bit closer. We tried to be open-minded to the idea of bi-luminescence, to be aware of the glow that bugs give off. Some people call the glow an aura, and we can't see it, but the fish can. It's something like the idea of a firefly, but not that intense. We get that shine, that aura, by using glass-bead patterns. We probably catch more fish on bead patterns than on anything else. And those aren't brass beads, they are glass.

And during big hatches having a fly that may be just a tad different makes all the difference in the world.

Q: Is that a difference for the better or for the worse?
Gomez: Better, because if the fly has a little shine to it, then it's going to be more attractive to the fish. We use golds, reds, greens, whites, clears—anything that has fire in them. When I first started designing and making flies with the glass beads I had to shop for them in craft shops and Wal-Mart, but now you can buy some that are specifically made for fly tying that will slip over the arch of the hook. But I still shop around various places for them. I have glass-bead patterns all the way down to size 26 now.

I place the beads in different places for different imitations. With worms I put the bead in the middle to give it segmentation, in Chironomids at the head of the fly and in mayflies I put the bead over the thorax. I even do some flies now with a scintilla bubble tied above a dubbed thorax. Looks just like a scintilla bubble, that pocket of air that *Baetis* and midges use when they're emerging, to help them rise to the surface.

Q: How responsible are you, personally, for all those strange fly patterns on the San Juan?
Gomez: Very responsible. When I first started tying for the shop I was doing Disco Midges, WD-40s and the usual stuff like that. When I first started going into the glass it was about the same time that Orvis came out with the brass-bead patterns. Then, after I was having good luck with them Todd [Todd Field, then a San Juan guide] suggested that I put them in the shop. I said, "Don't you think they look like earrings, though?" He said, "Stock them anyway. They're working great." Still, a lot of customers look at them ask if they're for catching fish or for catching people.

But a lot of other people come in and tell how they've taken them to other places—like Montana and back East—and did great with them. You'd be surprised at how many people stock up now and take those glass-bead patterns to other parts of the country.

When I went into the bi-luminescence the glass beads were the key. They do catch fish, and a lot of fish. I think that glass beads will really catch on and there'll be an explosion of them all around the country in the next couple of years.

Q: For the bi-luminescence do you use anything other than glass beads?

Gomez: Oh, yes. You can do it with Krystal Flash, like the Desert Storm pattern. You could also use Z-lon, Antron or any of the shiny yarns. Wrap it over the body, or over the wingcase. The glass beads just give off that fire, though, and give a little more to it.

Tiny Flies

Q: People who know what they're doing on the San Juan use smaller nymphs than folks use elsewhere, don't they? Why is that?

Gomez: One thing about the San Juan is that it has a huge population of Chironomids, which are real small. They'll run anywhere down to size 28s or smaller. We have a midge that comes off the river that has to be at least a 38. And when they're on the surface, fish will sit there and slurp them one at a time. And it's so small you can't imitate it. Last year we had a lot of big hatches of those.

Q: Do you fish any kind of cluster patterns with those midges?

Gomez: That kind of midge doesn't tend to cluster. We do have some bigger midges that are size 20 and 22 that do cluster, and I've seen clusters as big as quarters.

But to answer your question about the size of the flies on the San Juan, we use small flies because the natural bugs are small. But, as I've said, people have done well with my small glass-bead patterns in places where people ordinarily use bigger flies. For instance I've had people who've fished Cherry Bombs in size 24 or midges in size 26 in Montana and have done extremely well. And in Montana, a size 18 or 20 is considered a small fly. Maybe that's because there are a lot of really small naturals in those other waters too, and people just don't ordinarily try to imitate them.

Pattern Selection

Q: In your own fishing, do you tend to use a lot of patterns or just a few favorites?

Gomez: I use a lot of flies. A fly pattern doesn't just come on the scene and have the fish burn out on it. For instance, take the Brown Eyes pattern—which is a caddis emerger with a gold glass bead. The fish will eat that every summer during the caddis hatches. Every pattern has its time and can always repeat itself. So I keep going back to the old patterns as well as developing new ones.

By old patterns I mean WD-40s, Flashy Backs and your basic old San Juan Worm. The Worm always has its time on the river. I actually believe that 90 percent of the fishes' diet on the San Juan is worms. They're so abundant in the river and I think that's what gives the fish their girth and size.

I use the San Juan Worm in a real variety of colors, all the way down to a lime green and a purple. Purple is a real good color.

Q: It sounds like bass fishing, doesn't it?
Gomez: Sure does. I've even gone into using Rattletraps in leech patterns. It's the little glass bead with BBs inside that bass fishermen use inside their plastic worms. They click and rattle in the water and the noise attracts trout. The Rattletrap works extremely well. You can use them in Woolly Buggers and Rabbit Hair Leeches. It's pretty much a new thing that I'm doing. You buy the Rattletraps from the Bass Pro-Shop. I've used them in leech patterns in reds and purples. One of our guides ties a violet Woolly Bugger that works extremely well.

Future of Fishing

Q: Do you have any ideas about the future of the sport that you'd like to share?
Gomez: I always tell people to get involved with Trout Unlimited. They're the only organization there is that's really out to protect the sport, and I think endangered species could be the end of the trout fisheries. In the past couple of years we've gone into the low flows on the San Juan because of the squawfish, which is an endangered species. The low water hasn't hurt us yet, but if they keep it up it could change the habitat of the San Juan quite a bit and the river could change drastically in the next few years. In addition to protecting endangered species, we have less and less habitat for trout due to irrigation, water conservation and other things.

Look at Lee's Ferry. High flows really hurt that fishery, and the low flows up on the Madison caused whirling disease to come in. That low flow stresses the fish out, and it seems that's when the whirling disease comes in and attacks the fish. So far, we don't have any trouble with that here, but if they continue the low flows, who knows? Low flows here congest the fish, and the river's loaded with fish. If you get too many fish in one small area you could induce the disease.

Only as Crowded as You Make It

Q: Do you have any final words of wisdom that you'd like to share?
Gomez: One thing I'd like to say is that the San Juan is a river that's really crowded, but it's only crowded in certain spots. When you fish it, don't be afraid to venture away from the riffles and move downstream. It has a lot of good fishing for several miles below the dam. People tend to crowd up out there, but the guides, even on busy days, don't have problems finding places where there's nobody else fishing. All you have to do is look for them.

The myth about the San Juan being crowded is just a myth. Don't be afraid to move away from other people. There's plenty of good fishing. It's only as crowded as you make it.

Thomas J. Knopick

Where to reach him:
> Duranglers Fly Shop
> 801-B Main Street
> Durango, Colorado 81301
> Phone: 970/385-4081

Professionally guides now: Yes

Homewaters: "At one point I
would have said my homewater
was the Dolores, at another time
I'd have said it was Florida and now I'm starting to be more partial to the
Animas. Then at another time back there it'd have been the San Juan.
The area in general would be my homewaters, including all those that
I've mentioned."

Born: 1956 in Kansas

Came West: In 1975, when moved out to Fort Collins, to go to Colorado
State University. "For the start of my junior year. After that I went
down to northern New Mexico around Taos, then up here to
Durango."

Guiding history: Been guiding since 1983. Has guided in Colorado, and
mostly in the Durango area.

Why lives in Durango, Colorado now: "The primary reason is the fishing.
But also it's just a great, beautiful part of the West."

Present fishing business affiliation: Duranglers, a fly shop in Durango,
Colorado. He and John Flick are co-owners of that shop and another
Duranglers shop on the San Juan.

John W. Flick

Where to reach him:

Duranglers Fly Shop

801-B Main Street

Durango, Colorado 81301

Phone: 970/385-4081

Professionally guides now: Yes

Homewaters: "When we started out almost all of our trips were on the San Juan. Now it's a lot of water around here. That's because the quality of the water for fishing has improved so much since then. Now it's about 60 percent San Juan. My answer is pretty much the same as Tom's, and I love the Piedra, too. It's about 40 miles east of here. There's also the Los Pinos and the La Plata."

Born: 1956 in Kansas.

Came West: In 1975. "Tom and I were in pre-forestry in Kansas State. We transferred to Colorado State. After college I went to Honduras."

Guiding history: "We opened Duranglers in 1983 and that's when I started guiding here."

Why lives in Durango, Colorado, now: "We have eight months of fairly consistent good fishing. We can get 60 degree weather just about any timehere. You go north and we've got 14,000-foot peaks, and lots of them and you go south and there's high desert."

Present fishing business affiliation: A co-owner of Duranglers, Durango, Colorado.

John Flick and Tom Knopick operate Duranglers, the well-known fly shop in Durango, Colorado. The shop is large and well-stocked. There is another, smaller, Duranglers shop alongside the San Juan River, near Navajo Dam, New Mexico. The interview took place in the back room-office of the Durango shop.

Though not without humor, the interviewees were pretty serious types, especially on the subject of fishing. Both have been guiding for many years and both have a hands-on involvement with the shop.

Talking to them, I sensed a true partnership of two people who share a passion for fishing, the intensity of which focuses on the sport both as a daily pleasure and as an everyday joint economic enterprise. They've worked hard together and have something to show for it.

After most of my questions there was a hesitation before either wanted to answer, each waiting to give the other partner first shot. The clear impression was that of a partnership built on respect and long association, resulting in a similitude which excludes competition between the partners. Throughout the interview there was no difference of opinion between Flick and Knopick, only varying degrees of enthusiasm in their agreement.

Both the interviewees stayed in the room for the duration of the interview, which lasted the whole of a January morning. Had it not come to a timely end, though, Tom Flick would have concluded it, I believe. He was anxious to get headed down to the San Juan for an afternoon's fishing. And that lent support, of the most persuasive sort, to the statement that the Juan is a year-round fishery.

Question: *What's the best way to locate a good guide in a new fishing area?*
Flick: I'd say to go into your local fly shop and ask if they know anybody there who's good. We're a pretty tightly knit bunch, so chances are they'll have some good ideas. But don't just pick somebody out of the Yellow Pages, then hire them on the basis of how they sound on the phone. We know who the better guides are, and who they aren't, in other areas.

Selecting a Guide

Q: So if a person walked into your shop in Colorado and said they were headed for someplace in Montana, then could you come up with guide recommendations?
Flick: You bet, and we do it a lot. Any good fly shop does. And it has nothing to do with any commission basis, we just want to make sure he gets a good guide so he has a good experience there.
Knopick: And don't forget the World Wide Web. You can get on the net these days and search for fly fishing and get information about guides for just about any area. That's becoming a better source of information all the time.

Favorite Type of Client

Q: What kind of folks do you prefer to guide?

Flick: One of my favorite kind of clients is the person who has a lot of desire to learn but doesn't have a lot of expertise yet. Even if they've never held a fly rod in their hand before.

Knopick: I agree with John. You can see that sparkle in their eye, that grin on their face at the hooking of fish or even making a good cast. To me that's really rewarding.

I enjoy rank beginners too, if they're out there for the right reason. If they're fly fishing just because it's a fad, and if they just want to go back home and say they've been fly fishing in the West, then that person isn't an enjoyable person to guide.

It's overused, but if the person is haunted by waters, if being out there is a place they'd like to be, then a beginner is awesome.

Least Favorite Clients

Q: What is your least favorite kind of client?

Knopick: Cocky. A guy that knows everything but really doesn't. At the end of the day driving home you wonder why the guy paid you to be there. Maybe you've gotten him into the prime honey hole, right in the bucket, and you tell him to make this kind of cast and that kind of mend, and he says, "No, that's not the way I do it," or maybe, "That's not the way another guide told me to do it." He doesn't really want your advice, your input, and that's what a guide is there for.

Flick: I go back to what I said before. If he's not there to learn, if he's just there because it's the thing to do, then I can't teach him anything and at the end of the day he's no better than when we started.

And as for the guy who knows it all, I've seen it a hundred times. Two or three guys come out fishing, and one of them knows it all. He's been everywhere and he's fished for everything, so he doesn't listen to the guide. And at the end of the day who's caught the most fish? The beginner, because he's been listening to the guide, learning and applying what he's learned. The guy who's fished a lot before has the attitude that he doesn't need to listen to the guide; he's thinking, "This is the way I do it."

Knopick: Another kind of undesirable client is the one who has been brought along by somebody else and doesn't want to be there. It could be a husband bringing his wife, a father bringing his son or just a guy bringing along a buddy. If that person is there for the other person, like a wife being there because she thinks her husband wants her to be, then that's not a fun situation.

Years ago I had a husband and wife fish with me. They'd fished together all over the world for 35 years. While we were rigging up he came up to me and said, "This trip's mostly for her, so I want you to spend most of your time with her and put her into fish. She loves to fish but doesn't get to do it enough."

About five minutes later, she comes over to me and says, "Tom, there are some things you need to know about today's trip. I've been out with more guides than days that you've guided. And the only reason I'm out here is for my husband. I hate to fish. If you follow my rules the day will go fine. The rules are: I really don't want your company, I don't wade deep and I won't touch fish. Take off my fish, leave me alone and we'll all have a really fun day out there, Tom."

Q: So did you have a fun day?

Knopick: I didn't really enjoy it. I knew that she didn't enjoy it, and I knew that for 35 years this guy had been bamboozled into thinking that she loved to be there and catch fish. That's a real awkward position for a guide to be in. It makes a great story, but it wasn't a fun situation out there.

Line Control and Drag

Q: Switching over to fishing technique, what common errors do you see people make?

Flick: Line control while the line's on the water. In the first place, people are unaware of the need to manage line on the water. Maybe they've never even heard of mending line. My Dad, for instance, has been fly fishing forever but it wasn't until about 10 years ago that he understood what a mend was. He was a cane rod, wet-fly fisherman all his life, and what you do with wet flies is throw them out there and let the current drag them around the corner until the fish hit 'em. You don't worry about drag. And that technique still works today. A good dragging Trude during a caddis hatch is an amazing pattern. During a caddis hatch you can have too good a dead drift. The guy with the poorest drift usually catches the most fish.

But knowing you have to slow that fly down in a nymphing or dry-fly situation is something most people just don't understand.

Knopick: Most people just don't have an understanding of the relationship between the water and the line. I think John would agree that mending of the line is the most misunderstood concept in fly fishing. First of all, I don't think people know why they're mending. We see it all the time. You put a guy in a spot and tell him he needs an upstream mend. Then he moves down to another spot where the currents are totally different and he's still mending upstream.

John and I try to teach people how to manipulate the fly line. Is it an upstream mend or a downstream mend? Do you need a mend at all? But there are a lot of fishermen who just automatically put an upstream mend in their line without even knowing why they're doing it, except that sometime, some-place, someone told them to do it.

Flick: Once you teach a beginner to mend they often think they have to mend every time they cast.

Q: What other mistakes do people make?

Flick: One common mistake is that people think they have to wade in before they make a cast. But we catch fish standing up there on the bank without ever getting our feet wet because they're up close. People spook a lot of fish walking through them to get to some other run where they think there might be fish.

Knopick: It's like the grass is always greener over there.

Distance Casting Not Important

Q: How important do you consider distance casting?

Knopick: Not very important for most situations. You can be a real poor caster and still catch a helluva lot of fish if you've got good line control and understand your drifts. That's probably why we mention the line control and mending first.

There are some basic flaws in casting that a high percentage of fishermen have. But the worst place to try to learn how to cast is while you're fishing; you've got so many distractions.

Flick: Another common error is people keeping their line up in the air, doing too much false casting. You catch birds up there but the fish are all in the water.

Knopick: They see it on TV.

Flick: I teach them that if you don't have to false cast, then don't false cast. When you're fishing dry flies you might need to false cast two or three times occasionally to dry your fly, but you see people false casting four or five times, or even more.

Knopick: That's a mistake that the more experienced fishermen make rather than beginners.

Another potential problem guides have to deal with in experienced fishermen is that they try to cast too far. The farther you cast the harder it is to control the drift. Back to your mending. You get a guy who's trying to dump out 40 or 45 feet of line, then he loses control of his line and he's going to catch fewer fish. While if he'd shorten up, or wade out a little bit farther or reposition and fish 20 or 25 feet of line he'd probably catch more fish.

Sometimes you need a long cast, then it's good to be able to do it. But most fishing is short and accurate.

Importance of Observation

Q: If you could come up with a few rules for people to follow to improve their fishing, what would they be?

Knopick: Observation.

Flick: Yeah, observation is number one. Don't step into that water until you know what's going on.

Q: Observing what?

Flick: Bug activity, fish activity, water currents, turning over some rocks, deciding where to stand to fish—there is a lot to check out before even tying on a fly.

Bringing Fish In

Q: What do you teach people about landing fish quickly? Or do people even know that you should try to land fish quickly?

Flick: People let their fish run way too much. They give them line when they're running. They love to hear that reel screaming, you know. You have to break off a lot of fish to find out how much pressure you can put on that fish and not break him off. Sometimes people will say, "You landed that fish so quickly and all day you've been yelling at me, 'Easy, easy, easy'." It's just a matter of having learned where that pressure point is. And it's a matter of tippet strength, current, size of fish; all that enters into it. The underlying principal is that you can put an amazing amount of stress on monofilament as long as it's steady, but sudden impact will break it relatively easily.

Knopick: As many good fish are lost by being too easy on the fish as being too hard with them. Being too tentative, allowing the fight to go on too long makes it more likely that bad things can happen like the hook pulling out. And the more line that goes out the more chance the fish has of breaking you off.

Sure, you can make mistakes being aggressive with the fish, but once you get a feel for what you can and can't do, then a person who plays a fish aggressively will tend to land more fish than the person who is too timid. The fisherman has a lot of control over what happens, and he should be the boss.

One thing you can do is lower your rod and put a lower angle of pressure on the fish. He's more likely to follow your lead, go where you want him to go, if you don't have an 'up' angle of pressure that's trying to bring him up to the surface.

Q: How about nets? Do you use them?

Flick: In a boat we use the big nets that are more like a rubber basket, but wade-fishing I don't use one unless I'm in real fast current using a light tippet.

The most common mistake I see in landing fish, though, is people trying to go to the fish instead of letting the fish come to them, whether or not they're using a net. You make the fish come to you by pointing your rod back over your shoulder.

Expensive Tackle

Q: What mistakes do people make in selecting the tackle and equipment they show up with? Do they spend too much on some things and not enough on others?

Knopick: We've got some good fly shops out there now, and for the most part people come well outfitted. They're coming with all the right stuff. We see some guys trying to save money and show up with a poor rod and that's going to make it harder for them to learn fly fishing. These days, though, you can spend $100 and get a good graphite rod, and before that wasn't the case; you had to spend a lot more to get a decent one. If a guy tries to do it for $29 it doesn't work.

Flick: And there are some people who show up over-outfitted. You don't need an Abel reel to play a 12-inch trout. But with most of those people, that's what they want and they can afford it. It's a personal choice and none of our business if they want to have the most expensive fly rod and the most expensive reel, even though their skill level may not allow them to use that kind of equipment to its potential.

Selecting a Reel

Q: In the waters around here what kind of reel can a person get by with and still be adequately equipped?

Flick: A single action click and pawl. You don't need a disc drag. For a big fish we'd prefer a disc drag, but you could get by okay with a click and pawl reel if it's high quality.

Knopick: A click and pawl can be used by someone who's used to using it and knows how to use it correctly. Maybe somebody's been using a Hardy Marquis forever and knows how to palm the rim, and that's fine.

For me, it doesn't make as much difference what kind of drag system it is as much as whether it's smooth. And maybe even above and beyond that, durable. I want a reel that I can pound on a rock and it'll still work.

Selecting a Rod

Q: As to rods, how critical do you consider lengths and weights?

Flick: I like a longer rod, maybe 8 1/2 or nine feet at least. Probably not over nine feet, but not as short as eight feet. It can be lightweight, though. Of course, if you're fishing small creeks, which we do a lot of, then you can fish a seven- or 7 1/2- foot two- or three-weight.

Knopick: I'd say we'd both probably agree that if a person fishing in our area, and probably throughout the West, if they only have one fly rod it needs to be nine feet and a five- or six-weight. Once they have that, they can specialize their equipment if they so desire and if they can afford it. Maybe they can then get a 7 1/2-foot three-weight particularly for fishing the creeks or to present a challenge to themselves.

Downstream Dries

Q: In your own personal fishing techniques are there any things that you do

61

differently than commonly accepted techniques? Any tricks of the trade that you use?

Flick: I fish dries downstream. And that wouldn't go over in England. But we fish a lot of downstream drifts with dries, whether they be midges or little *Baetis* patterns. That way we can present the fly to him rather than presenting the leader first.

Knopick: That's a spring creek technique, and the San Juan or the Dolores can be a lot like fishing a spring creek. A lot of people aren't aware of the value of fishing dries downstream.

Nymphing the San Juan

Q: When you're nymphing do you ordinarily fish more than one fly?

Knopick: On the San Juan I think most of us use two or three flies.

Flick: I use two, but I've never used three. I know some guys who put a Christmas tree out there when they're fishing the San Juan. I've seen guides on the San Juan who had their clients fishing up to six flies at once.

But when you fish more than one fly, you do give the fish a choice of patterns, and you're fishing more than one level in the water.

Q: I've heard the San Juan described as being a place with big fish, tiny flies and huge crowds. Do you agree with that?

Knopick: That's a fair comment. It wasn't always like that. John's been fishing the San Juan since 1969 and the first year I fished it was 1979.

A small fly there used to be a size 18. The entomology of the river's changed subtly. But midges aren't necessarily smaller today than they were before. We used to tie up a short-shank Hare's Ear without a tail in a size 18. That was a midge pupa and the only midge pupa you needed. They weren't a good tie from the standpoint of imitation, but the fish ate them like crazy. But because of the pressure the fish are extremely well-conditioned as to what's going on. So they've seen that pattern and don't want to do it again. So the imitations have got to be more accurate—size, color, shape, the whole ball of wax—than what they were before.

Having daily fishing pressure, 365 days a year, will change a fishery.

Avoiding the Crowds

Q: But if a person knows what he or she is doing, can big crowds be avoided on the San Juan these days?

Knopick: I hope to do it today. Today's January 15, a Saturday and the weather is beautiful so there'll be quite a few people fishing it. If that same January 15 were on a Saturday and it's snowin' and a blowin' and it's nasty weather, then you can pretty much have any section of the San Juan to yourself. So you can avoid people by fishing it at the least desirable times. And it's a great experience to be out there when the snowflakes are the size of a half dollar.

And at any time of year there are fish all over that river. Most people fish in certain sections. There's a lot of water that people typically don't fish because they don't know it's there or it's a little farther to walk. The San Juan is a classic example of what I call the herd mentality. One fisherman goes to a place, then a second one does, then there are four of them so the next ten people who show up think that's where all the fish are so they go there. So you have a herd of fishermen out there. Just don't join that. Explore the water, find new places. You can find those uncrowded spots if you look for them, even when it's crowded. It's getting more difficult to do all the time, though.

But of course fishing in this area isn't just the San Juan. There is such an abundance and variety here. Everything from more high mountain streams than you could fish in a lifetime to mountain lakes and small and big freestone rivers. All that, in addition to the famous tailwaters, the San Juan and the Dolores.

The Future of Fishing

Q: Leaving the San Juan and environs behind us, what do you think the future of the sport is?

Flick: We've seen, obviously, a tremendous growth in the industry since we started in business. It's changed a lot. I think what we need nationwide is more quality regulated type of water. People in the West are still fishing the Green, the Bighorn and the San Juan.

But there's a lot of other water out there. In Colorado, for instance, we have 3,000 miles of fishable trout water and less than 500 miles have any regulations on them. We need more regulated water to take the pressure off the well-known rivers.

Most of the people going out fishing today think they've got to catch big fish, and lots of them. There are places like the San Juan where you can do that, so there's a lot of pressure. But some people—like ourselves, some of the guides and my Dad—say, "Hey, I'm going to go up here on Cascade Creek with my #10 Royal Wulff and catch six-inch brookies all day long, not see anybody, and I'm happy."

If we had more water that is just better than it is now, even if it's not as good as the San Juan, people might spread out more in their fishing. Then we could take pressure off some of these rivers and we won't hear that about the San Juan anymore—big fish, small flies and big crowds.

One problem is with the Fish and Game here in Colorado. A lot of the people in the department have an out-of-date fishing mentality. Their philosophy is that people came to Colorado to catch and keep the Colorado Rocky

Mountain rainbow trout. That was the old fishing philosophy and it was a good one way back then. Today, because of more anglers and more people, we can't let everybody catch and keep eight fish a day. We have to reduce that. And Colorado is very ancient in their techniques. They still think they can do it by raising these sickies, these catchables, throw them in the river, let people take them home and everybody's happy.

I'm not saying there's not a place for put-and-take fishing, or bait-fishing. But they need to bring the balance of that kind of fishing into perspective with fly fishing and stream management ideas of today rather than what it was 30 years ago. You could have the fishing wide open in those days. But now there are just too many people, and too many fishermen for that.

Knopick: There are some positive things, too. There are more people out there who believe in the catch-and-release philosophy. And where there isn't catch-and-release, at least they're limiting their kill. Just because the regulations say you can keep eight fish, they don't feel like they have to keep eight fish. More people are starting to understand that we have to conserve the resource. We have fishermen more educated in conservation than we did five, 10 or 20 years ago. More people know how to release the fish, for instance.

Flick: Not to brag too much, but I think that a good share of the increased education of the common angler today is from guides all across the West. I think good guides are the best teachers out there.

Q: That pretty well ends my questions, but is there anything you'd like to add?
Flick: I'd just like to say that a person should be out there for the right reasons. If you're not out there fishing for the right reasons then maybe you should take up golf.

Jennifer Olsson

Where to reach her:

P.O. Box 132

Bozeman, Montana 59771

Phone: 406/587-5140

Professionally guides now: Yes, in Sweden. Occasionally conducts group fly fishing schools and adventures in both the U.S. and Sweden.

Homewaters: Spring creeks near Livingston, Montana; the Gallatin River and Yellowstone Park waters; the Idsjöströmmen (of the Gim River), Sweden, from May through August

Born: 1959

When started fly fishing: At age 12

When came West: Came to Montana immediately after graduating from Vassar College in 1981.

Publications and videos:

Author: *Cast Again: Tales of a Fly-Fishing Guide*, Lyons & Burford (1996).

Contributor to the anthologies: *A Different Angle*, Seal Press (1995);

The World's Best Trout Flies, Boxtree Limited (1994);

Uncommon Waters, Seal Press (1991).

Columnist for Fiske Fîr Alla, Sweden.

Video: Hosted, "Women & Fly Fishing," (Miracle Productions, 1997).

From the beginning of my interview with Jennifer Olsson it was apparent that I was in the presence of a bright, witty and articulate woman who holds her opinions strongly. Even though she deals with serious subjects seriously, she appears to view the world through the lens of a memorable sense of humor. So there was a lot of laughter throughout our conversation and it was obvious that she, like most top-notch guides, is good company as well as a good teacher. Her sense of whimsy was evident before I even knocked on her door; she keeps a wooden bear on her front porch, near the door, that would draw a chuckle out of Scrooge.

We talked in the living room of her home in Bozeman, Montana. She lives in Bozeman with her husband, Lars-Åke Olsson, in a large and comfortable house located in a southern addition to the city. These days, she said, they spend much of each summer in Sweden.

Our interview, which was on a spring afternoon, terminated on schedule when time came for Jennifer to drive off to pick up her son, Peter, from school. I then had an opportunity to chat with her husband, Lars. He manages, guides and teaches fly fishing (flugfiske) on a section of the Gim River in Sweden and has introduced catch-and-release there, to the amazement of the local Swedes. Just now, he says, are they coming to appreciate the advantages of not killing the fish.

Question: *You do your guiding out of Bozeman. Are you a native Montanan?*
Olsson: No, I grew up in California, at least until I went away to college. As soon as I graduated, though, I came directly to Montana.

Coming Back to Montana

Q: What drew you here? The fishing?
Olsson: In part, but probably it was the fishing more than I realized. My father's mother and father were Montanans. My grandmother was born in Livingston in 1901 and her name—wonderfully enough—was Erie Montana McLaren. So this is a retreat back to my roots, and fishing is a part of it.

My family used to come here to fly fish when I was a kid. My mother died when I was 12, and as sort of a recovery my father would take us on great vacations here in the summertime. I used to fish with him on the lower Madison, near a place called the Channels area.

Q: Did your father get you started in fly fishing?
Olsson: Yes, and when I was 14 he and I went to a Fenwick fishing course in West Yellowstone. When we'd fish together he had the philosophy that he'd show me a few things but that I'd need to figure it out for myself. He wasn't going to stand there all day and baby me. And that was fine with me.

Q: You started guiding back in 1985, when there weren't as many women guides as now. What got you into guiding?

Olsson: I helped run a fly shop with my first husband and discovered that I enjoyed teaching people to fish. Next, I went out to New York and took the casting course given by Joan and Lee Wulff. I spent a couple of days with them when the course was over and we talked at great length as to whether I was good enough to teach casting. I felt complimented because they asked me if I wanted to come back and teach in their school. But I came back to Montana and started teaching and guiding here. Then I passed the state exam and became an outfitter.

Favorite Clients

Q: Speaking as a professional guide, what is your favorite kind of client?

Olsson: One who asks questions. I love questions. You can ask me questions all day and that makes me really feel good. I want to know what you want to know, so I can see if I know it.

I like enthusiasm and I like for a client to trust me and to follow my directions. These things are real important to me. And I like clients who can enjoy themselves. I like clients who try, whether or not they can do it. I like clients who like to stop and rest and who sometimes want to talk about anything but fishing.

I like for people to be happy, whether it's a five-inch brook trout or a 20-inch rainbow. I like clients who like to fish, who want to be there.

Q: What about fishing skills? Are you just as happy if the client is holding a fly rod for the first time?

Olsson: Oh, yeah. That's my specialty. It's fine with me if they don't even know which end of the rod to hold. It's hard work, but I prefer it because I feel I'm most effective that way.

The Guide as Teacher

Q: So it's fair to say that you enjoy the teaching aspect of guiding?

Olsson: I do. Because I feel that when they're ready for the learning experience they're really hungry and I'm doing what I'm supposed to do. I'm delivering information that I've been trained to deliver. And they're getting what they wanted.

I love teaching and I love taking that fear away, if I can do that. Maybe it's that female nurturing thing where you want to take care of people. "I'll make it better, I'll fix you. You just listen to Mother here and she'll take good care of you."

You might say that I'm possessed by wanting to help people, wanting to have them enjoy what I teach them.

Hand-Me-Down Tackle

Q: What mistakes do people make in selecting the gear they show up with?

Olsson: People who've been fly fishing for five years or so—and who fish more than two weeks out of a year—usually show up with pretty good stuff.

But I see so many beginners, and often they've been given the hand-me-downs. And that's a disaster. Usually their fly rod and line combination is atrocious in that the rod is too heavy and the line is always too light. Even if the rod and line are matched, like a five-rod matching a five-line, the line's too light. They'd need a six-weight line on it. That's what I see most of.

I had a woman show up at one of my casting classes that I hold for women, and she had this rod she was really proud of. She said, "My boyfriend gave me this."

I held the rod and cast it, and I said, "Well, is this a serious relationship? Is he maybe seeing somebody else on the side?" And the terrible thing is that one day I met this fellow and he said, "Hey, I'm the one you said that terrible thing about to my girlfriend." I asked him, "Did you ever buy her some decent equipment?"

Q: Did he ever get her the good stuff?

Olsson: No. And he'd gone off and bought himself a Winston. But this hand-me-down idea just doesn't work, unless maybe the hand-me-down rod is an eight-and-a-half-foot Winston.

Overlining Rods

Q: Once they have the proper rod, what problems do people have when learning to cast?

Olsson: Most people's casting problems come from not being able to feel the rod bend with the weight of the line, and the greatest problem is matching the line to the rod. And I don't mean matching numbers. I mean finding the right line weight for the rod regardless of the weight marked on the rod. The first thirty feet of line length is what is weighed to determine the rod it should be paired with, but most people do most of their fishing at 20 or 25 feet. So the rod isn't bending enough, they can't feel it happening. It's too light and they try to fight it. They push hard and they can't feel the line.

But you put a seven-weight line on a five-weight rod and suddenly the rod is bending at 20 feet, 10 feet, 15 feet and they're feeling something happening. And then it starts to make sense to them.

So the first thing I do is overline the rod. Immediately. At least by one line weight. If it's a five-weight rod, then a six- or a seven-weight line goes on it.

68

Double Taper Lines

Q: Do you have any strong preferences as to line tapers?

Olsson: Yes, I sure do. I like double-taper line. Especially in teaching. Weight-forward line has that bullet head on the front, to 'punch into the wind'—whatever that means—then you've got this little skinny running line off the back of it. Everyone says that in Montana you've got to have a weight-forward. I've done tests on the weight-forward and double-taper lines, and there's not really that much difference in casting distance.

If, for instance, you're testing by casting as far as you can throw them and the weight-forward will go 90 feet, then the double-taper will go 87 feet. There's no big difference in casting distance. I think that's because of the good coatings they're using on the lines now.

But the difference is that when you have someone who's learning or somebody who's not comfortable with the rod or their timing's off, the double-taper stays very thick throughout the body of the line and you don't have the taper interfere with the casting. With a weight-forward line you have to shoot the line at your 35- or 40-foot mark or otherwise it will start to weaken the cast because the rod tip starts to hit that weaker running line and everything goes to hell.

In other words, weight-forward is just more trouble for most people to cast. Double-taper is heavier in the hand, you can feel it, it casts gorgeous, it's not slow—that's a rumor—if you keep your lines clean. It's also true that double-taper is easier to mend and handle on the water because you don't have that goofy little running line to deal with.

But mainly, double-taper is a much nicer line to throw. I teethed on weight-forward lines, so it was really hard to break me off of them.

Women's Rods and Equipment

Q: Some of the rod makers are starting to market rods specifically designed for women. How do you feel about standard rods not fitting women's hands?

Olsson: Rods fit everyone. Special rods are not needed for women. Although some women do have a small grip, it's very simple to solve that problem. You sand the cork handle down until it fits. You get a rod-maker to help you or you just take the sandpaper and work on it until it feels more comfortable in your hand.

The only potential problem with women and rods is the grip. Rod weight shouldn't be a problem. A trout rod weighs an ounce or two; we're not lifting anvils here.

Q: How about other equipment?

Olsson: Shoe sizes can be a problem for women. If she's about 5-foot two then she probably has about a size six shoe and she might have trouble finding wading boots. But with neoprene waders, for a couple of extra dollars she can call up Simms and they'll custom fit her, inseam, stocking feet and all. Neoprene is probably good for life, if she sends them back to have the feet replaced when they wear out.

With Gore-Tex, and the other baggy waders, they're baggy on everyone so they've got to fit you in there somewhere. And the baggy ones are comfortable.

Women's Image In the Sport

Q: I understand you to say that you have no real problem with the way tackle makers approach the women's market? Is that accurate?

Olsson: Not exactly.

First the industry needs to take women, and the professional women in the sport, seriously in their advertising before they're going to get their money. Then they can start fooling around with things like colors for women's vests. But they're doing this thing backwards. The image of women in the sport is much more important than, "Should we make the vest pink?"

When I look at a fly fishing magazine I don't see enough pictures of women in there. I don't see the little round New York woman that I took fishing last week, she's not in there anywhere. I see her husband, but she's not in there. I see models who look like they were called at nine o'clock that morning to get the shot done. I don't see the treatment of women in the sport the way I witness women in the sport to be. If they want to sell their products to women, quit fooling around with the lace collars. They can do that later. They're putting the cart before the horse.

I think one reason they think there's not a women's market is because most women can wear men's equipment and use men's tackle. I can fit into a man's wading boot and with my hand I don't need a special grip on a rod. But a lot of the manufacturers are trying to track the number of women customers by the amount of women's equipment that's sold. That's how they come up with statistics that just aren't accurate.

Mend and Mend Again

Q: Are there any rules you can suggest for the average fisherman to follow in order to improve her or his fishing?

Olsson: I could make a tape for them to play on a recorder in their pocket. I'd say, "Mend your line" in 20 second intervals. "Mend your line. Mend again. Cast again. Mend again. Mend. Mend. Cast again."

Q: Is that because people don't mend their line enough?

Olsson: No, they don't. Once I can get them out of the trees and in the water—Chapter Two—now we have to work that fly. And my job all day long is to say, "Mend. Mend again. Now you're dragging. Pick it up. Mend. Now it's under. Cast again." It's exhausting, but that's what I do. Because people love to throw it out there and wait for something to happen.

So I'd say that a big rule is to mend and don't let your fly drag. Try to put the fly in good places for fish and don't try to cast too far. Everybody wants to cast way over there somewhere.

I'll say, "Where are you going with that cast?" They'll say, "The fish won't see me this far away." I say, "But you won't see them either, so let's get closer."

Organize, Then Move

Q: Any other rules?

Olsson: The other thing I'd want them to do is to sort of organize the whole thing when they approach a stream. Figure out a way to cover the water in a methodical sort of way. Try to work your upstream casts first. Then you can do your cross-stream section. Then turn yourself around and start doing your downstream casting. Just cover all the stuff around you.

Then move. That's another thing. Move. Take two steps. That's another thing I tell people. "Take two steps. Now take two more steps." People are perfectly happy and will stand there all day and won't move. If you let them, they'll plant themselves and keep casting to the same target in the water over and over for 45 minutes. And they're thrilled to do it. They don't realize that after 10 or 15 attempts either they've spooked the fish, it's just not the right spot or their technique or presentation is wrong.

Wading Safely and Well

Q: What about wading? Do most people know how to wade?

Olsson: No. They don't know how to wade, and wading is something I had to learn about myself. I love wading and I'm not afraid of water. I love dancing around on rivers. But the problem is, that can be dangerous and I can't let clients imitate me. So I've learned to carry a wading staff and it's helped me a lot. I tell people they must be careful how they wade. You must not go in up to your chest; no fish is worth it. The more submerged you are in the water the less control you have over your movements.

You can comfortably wade in water up to your knees, and for many people that's enough. And when you use a wading staff you've got to use it on the upstream side. If you have it upstream you can lean against it. If the water is pushing you, you can lean right into it. If you put the staff downstream you get no support from it at all if you start to lose control. You'll just spin around on it. You'll fall. But I recommend that everyone have a wading staff in almost any kind of water.

Also, when you're wading, you don't walk scissor-step, like when you walk down the street. You should move your staff forward, bring the right foot (if that's the one closest to the staff) close to it, then drag along the other foot. Then just repeat that. I call it a step-drag kind of walking.

Bringing Fish In

Q: Do you have any suggestions about playing fish?

Olsson: That's a difficult thing to teach to clients who are new to fishing because when they hook a fish they become autistic. They can't hear me. They can not hear me. They literally shut me out. No matter what I say they'll usually break the first fish off.

What they do wrong is they won't let go of the line. I tell them to let go of the line, let the fish run and play him off the reel. But that's a lot to ask of a new fisherman. I tell them to hook the fish, then let go. I literally reach over and pry their fingers off the line. I have to like slap their hand so they'll let the fish run. They can't hear me, they can't see me. They don't know what's going on.

For the average fisherman, who has landed some fish, I find that often they don't know how to push and pull. They don't know how to give it time. They are in a crisis state and just want to reel the fish in and get it over with. And that's not what it's about.

I try to convey something like, "Now you're into Chapter Three. This is the whole reason you came today. This is the dance you're going to do now. If he goes left, you go right. If he goes right, you go left. If he goes upstream you've got to figure which rock he went behind. If he stops, take line in."

You have to wake up your senses. Ultimately, you have to feel what is happening at the end of that line, and the more you catch fish the more you know how big the fish is and how much pressure you can apply.

Pattern Versus Presentation

Q: Any other tips for the average fisherman?

Olsson: Learn your riseforms so you know what you're looking at. Most people don't recognize when fish are taking emergers. They think that adults are being taken off the surface. If you don't see the mouth open and you see a lot of heads and tails, and swirls, then they're taking an emerger or pupa. When they're taking emergers you don't want to throw an imitation of an adult out there. They might take it, but not as likely as an emerger imitation.

Another thing people do is blame the pattern. It's always the pattern. "What are they taking? What are you using?" I'm almost convinced now that it isn't what you're using, it's how you use it. And there's always the saying that a poor workman blames his tools. You have to understand how to fish, I mean how to float a drag-free dry. And you have to use other techniques for fishing emergers, nymphs, soft hackles and streamers. Knowing and using those techniques well is a lot more important than having just the right pattern on.

Q: Let's talk about your own fishing techniques. What kind of fishing do you like best?
Olsson: I love dry-fly fishing. If I could dry-fly fish every day I'd never nymph again as long as I live. That's probably because I'm better at dry-fly fishing.

I have to say that I've improved my nymphing a lot because I really forced myself to nymph a lot. I realized it was a weak spot.

Dry Flies and Long Leaders
Q: Any dry-fly tips you want to pass along?
Olsson: Long leaders. At least 10 or 12 feet of leader, and about a fourth of that is tippet. Actually, I'm very unscientific about that. I buy the Climax knotless leaders and once I've fished it and hacked away at the end of it I'll strip off a piece of tippet material—whatever length looks good—and tie it on. Whether the piece I tie on is a foot long or two feet long depends on how it's casting for me. If it feels a little sloppy I'll cut it back. If I can get away with a little bit longer, I will; if I can't deliver it well I'll cut back and re-attach the fly.

But I've learned that the long leaders are helping quite a bit with drag. I used to subscribe to the notion that, especially for learners, you should keep the leaders really short—like seven and a half feet. It gave them more control. But it also causes more drag, especially in dry-fly fishing. If I can get their skills up to casting a nine- or 10-foot dry-fly leader, then they get better results.

Parachute Adams' and Gold Bead Flies
Q: Do you carry a lot of patterns when you fish on your own?
Olsson: I have a lot of flies because I get gifts, and my husband is a fly tier and he has his own series of patterns that he's developed over the last 20 years. I've always had flies. It was like I was born with a box of flies.

But if you told me that the house is burning and that I should grab some fly patterns and get out then it would be a Parachute Adams. I catch everything on that stupid thing. That would be number one.

Q: What would be fly number two? Is there a number two?
Olsson: I don't know. I like to fish with beetles and ants, oddly enough. Because sometimes I can fish an ant like a midge cluster and they'll take it. I

love the Griffith's Gnat, but now I've found an ant pattern and it works better. For me any way. Just a black ant.

I used to be a big Woolly Bugger fan but I haven't fished a Woolly Bugger in two years. And I made a vow this year not to fish gold beads. I've sworn off of all bead patterns, for this year.

Q: Why the bad blood between you and bead patterns?
Olsson: Because it's not the game I want to play. Because the whole idea and the fun of this thing is to figure out what they're eating. What are the fish taking in their own environment. I don't spin-fish because I like the fact that I'm working with insects, working with this food source, that somebody a hundred years ago designed this pattern to imitate that food source. And there's all this history and art behind all that. And a gold bead is just augmenting that; sounds like smearing it with Chummin' Rub. It's defeating what I started out to do. Although it's a helluva lot of fun and a gold bead has saved the day on many a trip, especially with clients. But for me, it's not satisfying anymore. It's like, "Oh, I caught it on a gold bead. It doesn't count." You might as well give me an ultralight spinning outfit and I'll go for it.

So I'm doing a retro thing where I want to fish soft hackles and I want to fish nymphs without gold-bead augmentation to see if I can do it. I want to know whose skill is involved: mine or the fly tier's. And I'd like to think it was my skill that caused this thing to happen with me and this fish. But I love the fact that I'm out there trying to figure out what they're taking so that I can get in on it.

That's why, in my own fishing, I don't use gold-bead flies. They're so effective. I just feel better about fish I catch without a gold bead.

Q: Why do think they're so effective?
Olsson: I have no idea, but I sort of think it's the flash. Fish take for a lot of different reasons. One is curiosity. They don't have philosophical thoughts about things going by. It's either they're hungry or they're not. Or, they're bored and curious. Or, like a baby, they put everything in their mouth. They don't have hands so they can't touch and feel it then throw it away. They put it in their mouth and spit it out. They're always looking for food. So curiosity is probably why they hit those things. Or they're crabby. They keep seeing it go by, and they swat at it by biting it.

Soft Hackles, Upstream
Q: You mentioned soft-hackle flies before. Do they have a place in your repertoire?
Olsson: Soft hackles are gorgeous. I'm thrilled with them.

Q: How do you like to fish them?

Olsson: My greatest success with soft hackles is fishing them like an emerger. You don't weight them. You cast upstream, let the fly sink down, let it swing across and come up. That's usually when the fish hits it. It's a Leisenring lift. The fish love it. You're fishing it 12 to 15 inches from the surface that way. You can also put flotant on it and fish it on the surface. Another thing I do with a soft hackle sometimes is high-stick it, keep the rod tip up so there's no drag, just let it come through with no pressure on it.

Q: Anything else about your personal fishing?

Olsson: Over time, I've tuned in more to what fish are eating. I used to only just want to catch them. Now I really like to take the time to study the stream and figure out what they're feeding on.

Q: Then you tie on a Parachute Adams, right?

Olsson: I immediately put a Parachute Adams on. "Oh, I see what they're eating. A Parachute will work good."

Q: Seriously, do you fish that fly that much?

Olsson: All the time. I fish the Parachute Adams a lot. It's ridiculous. I think it's because I can see it.

And Lars has a fly he designed that he calls a Fluttering Stone. Every year I can't get enough Fluttering Stones for my birthday. I just love them. It's like a gigantic Griffith's Gnat only with blue dun hackle. More fish have taken that thing. It's so simple. The simpler the better. And it floats like a cork. It simulates the fluttering wings of an egg-laying female stonefly. And WHAM, they take that fly. I like to fish with simple patterns. Nothing too complicated. Nothing augmented. I don't want a little Flashabou.

Know How to Have Fun

Q: Anything else fishermen should know?

Olsson: They should know how to have fun. The motto of [my husband] Lars' fishing club in London is in Latin, but it translates into "There is more to fishing than catching fish." People should remember that. At least that's what I like to think about.

And practice. Practice your skills. Don't use a guide every time you go out. Also, when you are being guided get as much as you can from the guide. Listen to them, ask questions. You don't have to take all the advice, but listen to it—give it a shot. This person is there every single day. They do know something.

Most important, when you're out there enjoy yourself. Try not to take the office with you. Or your office behavior with you, either.

Women In Fly Fishing—No Longer an Oddity

Q: What problems do you think the sport is facing these days?

Olsson: The biggest problem I have with it at this point is the balance of representation for men and women. I think the sport is going to suffer financially until they acknowledge women as participants and as professionals in a more realistic way. By professionals I mean guides, speakers and authors.

I think it's time to quit treating women as an oddity. "As a special report: We've found a woman who fishes." They've got to stop doing that because it's really old and tiring. It's also not true. There's a woman guide in every valley in Montana, and it's more than ever in the history of the sport.

Q: Do you find that you have difficulties with male clients that a male guide might not have? Because of the attitude of the male client?

Olsson: I think male clients and male guides have a whole different set of conflicts. There's a lot of posturing when it's a male-and-male situation. I've had my own set of conflicts with male clients, but not like I've heard coming out of other boats. You've got these poor, sunstroked guides who've been working for 90 days and somebody gets in the boat and insults them and then all hell breaks loose. So it's real different, their posturing with each other is real different from the way they behave with me.

Where I find my difficulties isn't with clients, it's with the industry itself. It's in getting those jobs—speaking engagements, trade-show assignments, endorsements and it's going to take a while. But I think we're ready right now for women to be a part of the sport.

As a fly fishing professional, my concern toward manufacturers and magazine people isn't, "You bad guys are so mean to us." That isn't it. It's, "You're losing money, and in turn we're losing money. So why don't we get together and make money?" That's what I'm trying to point out.

Fly Fishing Magazines

Q: What steps would you suggest that fly fishing magazines take to change that situation?

Olsson: They should change their content and focus. For instance, I've wanted to write something about fishing with my son, and I've been told by magazines, "We don't want anything about a mother and child in this magazine." But that's a valid experience for me. That is a very important fishing experience for many women out there. It's how you write it. If you write this blubbering thing then everyone's going to throw up, but if you present it in a professional way it should be OK. After all, men write about fishing with their kids. It's a rite of passage.

76

This isn't affirmative action I'm talking about. There are some really great women writers out there, and if the magazines would put them on assignment you would get incredible outdoor pieces on fishing. But the magazines don't have the guts to do it. If they did then they'd get more of a variety of ads to support the magazine, for instance a yogurt company, or a lodge catering to families. I don't advertise in the premier fishing magazines because I can't reach women. And that's my focus.

Also, I think they've got to stop doing to women what they've done to men. They've made men in the sport into bachelors. Even if you're married, you're a bachelor as far as they're concerned. You're on your own, you're with the guys and there's no family life on those pages. I don't see my father's life there. He fished with me, my sister and his wife. And what I see coming in the magazine treatment of women is, "We'll treat you like bachelorettes, like another guy."

Fly Fishing Couples

Q: Do you see many people fishing as couples, a man and woman on the stream together?

Olsson: I've made a business in the last five years out of fishing couples. And I don't see couples represented in any magazines. Every day I see happy, retired couples fishing together on the river, but I don't see any of them in the magazines. I don't know why they're not allowing those images to come forth.

One of the myths is that men fish to get away from women. It's from the 1950s. That is not what I'm seeing. Oh my god, they're dying to be with their women. This is saving marriages. It's absolutely perfect for couples. It's the best thing that's happened for couples and I see nothing of that reflected in the pages of fishing magazines.

Last Words

Q: Jennifer, is there anything you'd like to add? Some last words of wisdom?

Olsson: When you asked me about problems with the sport I started off on my feminist slant. But I think the other problem with this sport is that there are more and more people who want to play. I think we have to be careful of how we treat the resources and how we treat each other on the stream. When we're out fishing we should be polite, friendly and co-operative. We're all in this together and there's a lot of us, so make room and communicate with people on the river in a positive way.

There's plenty of room, so try to come to the river with an attitude of co-operation and helpfulness. That would be a really good thing to keep in mind as the sport grows.

Larry Tullis

Where to reach him:

2588 South 900 East

Salt Lake City, Utah

84106

Phone: 801/466-3921

Professionally guides now: No

Homewaters: "Utah, Idaho and Montana are the main trout waters, but I fish from Alaska to Chile, too. Recently fished far eastern Russia."

Born: 1961, Provo, Utah

Grew up: States of Hawaii, Utah and Washington

Guiding history: Started guiding in 1983; guided on the Henry's Fork, Madison River and Yellowstone Park waters. Then guided the Green River in Utah and Alaska. Has done some guiding in Chile.

Publications and present fishing business affiliations:

Associated with Angler's Inn, Salt Lake City, Utah. Has a mail order business, Unique Fishing Products.

Author and photographer for *Green River* and *Henry's Fork*, the River Journal series, Frank Amato Publications, Inc;

Nymphs: Tying & Fishing, Frank Amato Publications, Inc.;

Small Fly Techniques and *Nymphing Strategies,* Lefty's Little Library of Fly Fishing, Odysseus Editions.

Larry's articles and photographs appear frequently in the fly fishing magazines and he's helped produce a TV fishing show, "Outdoor World."

My interview with Larry Tullis took place on a spring morning at the kitchen table of his home in Orem, Utah. Since then, he's moved up the Interstate the few miles to Salt Lake City.

Larry is a recognized author and photographer as well as a guide, and when I arrived he was sitting at his computer knocking out an article for a fly fishing magazine. He's a very gracious guy, and showed no impatience that the interview was cutting into his writing time.

From the get-go I knew I was sitting down with a person whose life was firmly focused on fishing and the outdoors. When our conversation wandered from my interview questions, it didn't wander very far. Larry is one of those lucky people for whom his work is his play.

Before the interview I'd seen pictures of Larry in one of his books, River Journal: Green River, *Frank Amato Publications, Inc. (1993). My impression was that my interviewee was going to be a somber fellow indeed. He even manages on page 18 of that book, to avoid smiling while holding a four-pound rainbow for the camera.*

That impression was all wrong. Larry is full of life, has an energetic mind and is a pleasure to be around. Nothing somber about him. Nothing, that is until my cameras came out. Then a somber Larry explained that he's a photographer who finds it really unpleasant being on the wrong side of the lens.

Question: Larry, how long have you been guiding?
Tullis: I started up on the Henry's Fork in 1983. Later I guided on the Green River in eastern Utah, and guided there for about five years. Then I worked up in Alaska for a couple of years, then down in Chile and some other places.

Q: Are there any ways in which your approach differs from that of most other guides, anything unusual?
Tullis: Not particularly unusual. I tend to concentrate more on nymphing and a lot of guides tend to stick with dry flies. My main emphasis, though, is to try to make the client an extension of myself, and of what I would do if I were the person fishing.

The Joy of Guiding Beginners
Q: Some guides resist guiding beginners, people who've never even held a fly rod before. How do you feel about guiding folks like that?
Tullis: I figure about 80 to 90 percent of the people I guide are beginners or close to beginners. So I think it's the guide's job to teach the person, starting with the basics—casting, mending, how to set the hook, play fish and so forth. I think it's a lot of fun even though it's real tough at first. They're tangling their line, hooking

their guide, thrashing the water up. But once they start getting dialed-in it's really satisfying to watch them catching fish and having fun. So I don't mind guiding beginners at all, really. Sometimes it's more fun than actually fishing myself.

Of course, it's also a lot of fun guiding someone who knows what they're doing but will listen to you, and really start working fish.

Drag and the Average Fisherman

Q: What mistakes do average fishermen commonly make, even after they've mastered the basics?

Tullis: As I said, I'm heavily into nymphing—especially small nymphs to selective fish—and the biggest problem I've found is people have a really hard time getting a natural drift. At least natural enough for my taste and to catch the selective fish. Most people always have drag on their fly. Either they're not concentrating on watching the indicator or they simply don't have enough slack line on the water.

Q: Is the lack of slack line on the water related to the casting or to line manipulation?

Tullis: It's related both to line manipulation on the water and to casting. I'm a big fan of a lot of small "S" curves. Most people cast, mend once and have one big "S" curve, which helps a little bit but they're still dragging. If you can get a bunch of those little "S" curves in your line that's the key because the little "S" curves allow the current to act on the line in a variety of ways and still drift the nymph or dry fly naturally.

If you have too much slack out there you have a hard time setting the hook, so there's a real fine balance between too much and not enough. But I'd say that 90 percent of fly fishermen don't put enough slack out on the water.

Q: How do you put those small "S" curves in the line?

Tullis: There's a variety of ways. You can wiggle cast or bounce cast, or what I do a lot is cast, mend, then wiggle out line and mend again so you're sort of mending and feeding line out at the same time. You're actually putting a little pile of slack right underneath your rod tip. A lot of people seem to have something against that, and they'll raise their rod to get rid of the slack so they can sort of feel what's going on, but you lose your natural drift when you do that.

On a lot of waters where I fish, like the Green River, if you have any tension on your line when you should have a dead-drift then forget it, the fish won't eat it. They're just too selective, and that's with both dries and nymphs.

Q: What about the average fisherman's casting? Do they cast far enough, or maybe too far?

Tullis: Most people don't have the ability to cast far enough. Not that they need to cast that far, but the ability to cast farther improves the accuracy of your shorter casts. And accuracy is real important in getting the fly to the fish.

The Tale of the Indicator

Q: What other problems do average fishermen have?
Tullis: Hook setting on nymphing. Most people don't concentrate enough. The fish these days, with catch-and-release, have been caught a lot and they have such fast reactions. They'll take it and spit it out very quickly, and I'd say that most people miss 80 percent of their hits. It's not so much a matter of slow reflexes of the fishermen, it's that they simply don't recognize strikes when they happen.

When they start, the clients are all looking for the indicator to go WHAM, and go racing upstream. It hardly ever does that except for a real aggressive fish.

Q: You mentioned using your indicator to tell whether you're getting a good drift. What's involved in that process?
Tullis: You can see the speed of the indicator relative to the speed of the bubbles or whatever else is floating near it. If the indicator is going faster than the bubbles you know you're getting drag. If it's going slightly slower than the bubbles then you know that your nymph's right down in the strike zone, the prime nymphing zone along the bottom where the water is slower than the surface.

And I find that a strike indicator is a lot more accurate than just watching the end of your line in judging the speed of movement relative to bubbles and debris.

Q: Then is it fair to say that if the indicator is moving at the same speed as the bubbles that the nymph isn't down deep enough?
Tullis: Generally, that's true. However, fish have varying sizes of strike zones and you may be in a strike zone even when the fly isn't on the bottom. But yes, it is true that if the indicator is not moving slower than the bubbles around it then the nymph isn't down on the bottom in what I call the prime strike zone.

And to me, that use of the indicator is as important as having your indicator tell you that a fish has eaten the fly.

Q: How far apart do you rig your indicator and flies for nymphing?
Tullis: I generally try to put the indicator 1 1/2 to two times the depth of the water. Usually two times the depth. I keep adding weight until I'm occasionally hitting bottom. Then I know that I'm right down in the zone I want.

I think that fine-tuning the weight on a leader is something a lot of people don't do. I think it's important.

Q: Should people be able to tell when they've hit bottom as opposed to missed a strike? Is there a way to tell the difference?
Tullis: It's hard to tell the difference at first. Then, after a while, you learn where your fly is compared to where you think the fish are going to strike. If the indicator constantly keeps going under but when you set the hook you get nothing, you know you're getting rocks. Then you've got to remove a little weight or put the indicator closer to the fly. Once you fine-tune it to the water you're fishing then you set the hook on anything that might be a strike.

Nymphing Rigs

Q: What kind of underwater rig do you like to use when you're nymphing? Do you use more than one type?
Tullis: I use probably a dozen different nymphing rigs. One that I use quite a bit around here, and in other water that have good gravelly riffles and runs, I call the bounce rig. You don't hear too much about it. I use an extra-long leader—about three times the depth of the water you're fishing—with a light tippet, usually 5X, with two droppers, with weight on the very bottom and a strike indicator up at the top.

Q: You put the weight on the bottom of the rig?
Tullis: Weight on the very bottom. What that does is put the flies immediately right down into the strike zone. And the bounce rig keeps it down in the prime strike zone for three or four times longer than the traditional strike indicator technique. Now the traditional technique works better for rocky runs and mossy bottoms, but the bounce method works quite well when you have a clean gravel bottom.

I generally rig each of the two flies on a four- or five-inch dropper, with the bottom dropper about 10 or 12 inches above the weight, and the upper dropper about 10 or 12 inches above the bottom dropper. That varies some, depending on the type of water you're fishing.

Q: Why do you prefer to use a dropper rather than tying the flies into the leader? Tying into the leader would be easier, wouldn't it?
Tullis: For this kind of rig I prefer to use droppers because, with the weight dragging behind, the current takes the dropper out in front of the leader so the fish sees the fly first before it sees the leader. In effect, the nymph is floating backward. I think you have a better chance of hooking selective fish that way than you would if the flies were inline.

And this method works best with small, unweighted nymphs. Size 14 to 24. Big nymphs generally tend to hang down and tangle more.

Q: Do you think that using two nymphs is more effective than just one?
Tullis: I sure do. I kept track one year while guiding, comparing people using one fly as opposed to two. They'd fish one for a while and I'd switch them to two. On the average they were getting about 35 percent more fish when fishing two flies even though they might be undoing tangles a little bit more. Another thing about fishing two is that you can find out more quickly what flies the fish are going for.

Start Fishing While Ashore

Q: Thinking of people fishing without a guide, are there some rules that you would give people to help them catch more fish?
Tullis: The first one would be to start with observation rather than jumping in the water and fishing. Most people get waist-deep in the water before they start fishing.

I think you should start fishing 10 feet before you even get to the bank. Start looking at the vegetation to see if there are some bugs that have been hatching that are underneath shady leaves and under logs. Then pick up a few rocks close to shore and see what nymphs are available. Or even better get an insect screen out and get a sampling to know what aquatic insects are in there at the moment. Put the net in the current and disturb the rocks upstream.

What I usually do is carry a little dish and put the flies I plan to use next to the naturals to see how close they come. Color to me isn't nearly as important as the size and shape of the fly. Once you get the size and shape down all you've got to worry about is natural presentation. For most streams that would be a natural drift right near the bottom for the nymphs or a natural drift right on the surface for dry flies.

As I said, the average person thinks he has to be waist-deep before he starts fishing, and there's a lot of places where the fish would actually be behind you from where you're standing. I look for fish along the shore. There may be some lying there in six inches of water.

I think a lot of people simply don't realize how many fish are in six to 12 inches of water. Sometimes 80 to 90 percent of the fish are up in the shallows, especially when little hatches are coming off, like midges.

Q: What other suggestions for the average fisherman?
Tullis: I like to tell people, "Think laterally." People usually think along one line: "What hatch is going on? I've got to imitate that hatch perfectly." I like to come in from a different angle sometimes. Like, considering what's going on

right now, what attractor fly would work good? Or if I'm going to be covering a lot of water, what suggestive type fly will look most like a variety of things that are available to the fish right now.

A lot of people get duped into thinking that you've got to match the hatch. That's kind of the byword nowadays. I think there's a lot of other things that trigger fish into striking other than precise imitation. Trout habits are one thing I write about quite a bit, and hunger is only one small part, and selectivity is only one small part, of what makes a fish take a fly.

Imprinting Hatches

Q: What things, other than selectivity, make a fish take a fly?
Tullis: One of my theories about trout I call "imprinting." The theory is that when a trout feeds on an item for a long time the fish keys on certain aspects of that particular insect. Those insects get imprinted on the fish's mind by conditioned response, by identifying it over and over again. For instance, if a trout feeds on mayfly duns for several days in a row, it will generally start keying in on one, maybe two, things about that insect that triggers a strike. Quite often it's the shape of the wing, the surface impression on the water from the legs, or something like that. Something that they can easily identify as their food.

If you use a fly that has that same trigger—a good wing silhouette or a good surface impression—then you're going to catch that fish. That's where I think matching the hatch, as we think of it, is lacking. My philosophy is that almost all flies have parts that are a suggestive imitation, something buggy that doesn't look like anything specific but a lot of things in general. Attractor flies are basically flies that have triggers on them that trigger fish into taking.

White wings are a good trigger, and so are brown hackle, peacock herl, flash, beads, Krystal Flash or something like that.

Imprinting is very important. It takes a long time for that imprint in the fish's mind to fade out. I've found as much as a month or two months after a certain hatch you have what I call parallel feeding activity, in which you use attractor flies that come close but don't exactly imitate an item that was hatching a month before that.

So if you know what they were feeding on a month before, can figure out what a faded imprint of that would look like and pick an attractor fly that would match that, then you're going to trigger some feeding activity from fish that aren't even feeding at the moment. When that fly comes into view, it matches the faded imprint and it triggers a feeding response.

The Importance of White Wings

Q: Can you give me some examples of attractor flies that you'd use for common types of insects that had hatched a month before?

84

Tullis: Royal Trude—a down-wing, white wing fly—works very well about a month or six weeks after the stonefly hatches are completed. In the spring, you've got lots of small mayflies and midges hatching; a month or two after that the small Royal Trudes and small Royal Wulffs work real good. Sizes 16 and 20. And little Humpies, tied with real light elk hair.

Fish that should be selective, that are feeding on something completely different at the time, will all of a sudden trigger on those little attractors. Something a little different but that kind of matches the imprint.

Q: You like the white wing for this kind of thing, don't you?
Tullis: I heard it described as the white mystique, people wondering why white works so well for trout. It just seems to trigger something. In trying to figure that out I came up with the theory that the imprint fades to white.

I've found that it happens in many places. You can go to almost any stream and catch trout by adapting the insect that was hatching a month before to a pattern with a white—or almost white—wing.

All this is something that you can't prove scientifically, but it's worked for me so many times in so many places that it's become a pattern of my fishing.

Use Streamers on Rising Fish

Q: You used the term "thinking laterally." Precisely what do you mean by that?
Tullis: Most people think on one line: fish are rising, put on a dry fly; fish aren't rising, put on a nymph. When you think laterally you look at it from different angles. Fish are rising, so think what else would work besides a dry fly. Most people would be surprised at how well streamers work on rising fish, for example.

Q: That's a surprising thing to hear. Not incredible, but surprising. Why would you use a streamer on rising fish?
Tullis: When selective fish get keyed in on one food item you can catch them on an exact imitation sometimes, but sometimes even then they can become very, very difficult. There are times when you can break that pattern with what I call "hatch- busters." Things that work other than the exact hatch that they're feeding on.

It's sort of like when somebody tosses you a baseball and says, "Think fast." You put a streamer in front of a fish that's doing something else, and basically you're telling him, "Think fast." He's either going to say, "OK, I'm out of here," or grab it. Like when you catch that baseball, only the fish uses his mouth, of course, for that same reaction.

Another fly that's good as a good hatch-buster would be a terrestrial. Even when the fish are feeding on, say, a blue-wing olive mayfly, you might throw a beetle out there. They like the taste of beetles, and they may be getting tired of eating the same old thing. They'll come up and grab something a little bit different that's not out of their realm of feeding. They recognize beetles and hoppers and they're opportunistic toward them. When they're there, they'll take them. Maybe when they're only eating one out of every 15 natural mayflies that come by, when an ant comes by, WHUMP, they've got it because they're opportunistic towards that.

There are some fish, though, that get so keyed in on a hatch that they'll ignore imitations of the natural they're feeding on. Early in a hatch a general imitation, like an Adams, might work as an imitation of the natural they're eating, but as they feed on the hatch more and more they gradually get more selective as to the imitation. That imprint on their mind keeps getting more and more defined. So later, at the end of a hatch, your imitation of that natural might not work with them, and that's when a hatch-buster is most useful.

I figure that the harder fish get to catch the more it means that you're not thinking of something. You need to look at it from a different point of view. And that's what I call lateral thinking. Would streamers work, would attractor flies work and if so which attractor flies? Or which hatch-busters might do the job?

The Tullis Wiggle Bug

Q: In your own personal fishing do you have any other techniques that are different from conventional techniques? Any tricks of the trade?

Tullis: One technique would be using a type of fly I developed—the Wiggle Bug. It's a streamer fly that swims like a minnow. It has closed-cell foam on the back and a diving lip on the front. It's basically a Woolly Bugger type fly that dives and swims from side to side as you retrieve it. This fly opens new opportunities because it appeals to the fish's lateral line. The fish can feel the fly just like they can feel other things in the water by their pressure waves, things like other fish or a person wading.

You can use this fly at night or in totally muddy water where they can't even see the fly. They can feel it because it's pushing water and creating a low-pressure wave.

Strike Indicators

Q: Any other techniques?

Tullis: This is by no means unique to me, but in heavily fished water I'll use a big dry fly as an indicator. That's because when trout are fished over a lot they become more selective and come to associate strike indicators with getting caught. Sometimes they'll actually interrupt their feeding to let a strike indicator pass by. It's a survival instinct. They move out of the way to let the indicator pass, then move back where they were and start feeding again.

Q: What kind of indicator do you prefer when you're not using a dry fly?
Tullis: Usually I use the molded Styrofoam, the kind that you break off a toothpick in the hole. I use various sizes and colors. The reason I use them is because it's easy to adjust them on the leader. A lot of people don't adjust and that's a big mistake. You should always adjust to the kind of water you're fishing, adjusting the indicator 20 or 30 times during the day.

As for yarn, I think you can see more subtle variations when fish take the fly, but they're more wind resistant and harder to cast for the average person.

Q: There are some folks who are purists and who consider using any indicator to be like using worms. How do you feel about that?
Tullis: That's fine. They just won't catch as many fish.

Q: It sounds to me as if you really prefer nymphing to dry-fly fishing. Am I right?
Tullis: Probably 75 percent of the fishing I do is nymphing. That's because I fish any time of day and not just during the hatches, and 90 percent of the time fish are feeding on nymphs. It's as simple as that. And even when they're feeding on dry flies I'll stick with nymphs or emergers right up until I feel there are more fish feeding on dry flies than there are subsurface.

The Why and How of Kick Boats
Q: Do you have any tips on equipment and tackle?
Tullis: Kick boats. I'm big into kick boats, the pontoon boats with the frame on top. I've been helping a half dozen companies design them, and the designs are now getting to the point that they're pretty good for drift-fishing rivers.

Q: I tend to think of those as rather iffy, not too stable on moving water. Am I wrong?
Tullis: In the past they were like that. You had to be pretty good at running white water to use the previous designs on moving water. But in the last couple of years the designs have been getting good enough to handle class III and class IV white water. That's assuming that the person knows how to run that kind of water.

Q: What is a kick boat exactly? What's the best way for a fisherman to use one?
Tullis: A kick boat has two pontoons, about 7 to 10 feet long. You propel them either with fins or oars. With a rocker design, you can spin them on their axis more easily to go between rocks and other obstacles. Doing that with fins leaves your arms free to fish and you can get into areas that drift boats can't

WISDOM OF THE GUIDES

get into. And you're fishing all day instead of taking turns with the oars. And remember, that in moving water—unlike a lake—you don't move backward when you're using fins; you're kicking upstream as the kick boat is moving downstream. Just like rowing on a river and facing downstream.

Q: When you use a kick boat do you primarily kick or primarily row?
Tullis: It depends on the water I'm fishing. On a big river like the Green River I primarily use fins and fish the banks, pull in the backeddies and I'm always fishing. It's like riding a bicycle; you don't even have to think about it after a while. Your feet take you wherever you want to go, and you let your hands do the fishing.

Then if you get into a situation where you don't have confidence in the fins, say in white-water rapids, then you kick your feet up on the footrest and grab the oars. With oars, a kick boat is twice as maneuverable as a drift boat. You can do incredible things with them through fast, rocky sections.

On still water, a kick boat is two or three times as fast as a float tube because you have so much less drag. You can literally do circles around a float-tuber. I think that kick boats are the future of fly fishing watercraft.

Favorite Fly Patterns

Q: In your personal fishing do you carry and use a wide variety of fly patterns, or do you find that you pretty well stick with a few favorites?
Tullis: I fall in the category where I carry a lot and experiment a lot, but I always come back to a few of my tried-and-true patterns that I've found to be effective either everywhere or in specific waters.

Q: What are some of those tried-and-true patterns?
Tullis: Well, some very simple dubbed nymphs. All they are is dubbing on a hook that's been brushed out and trimmed a little bit. Nothing else on it. I usually mix synthetics and natural materials to get a sort of translucent, buggy look. Like Antron and rabbit. Once you brush it out and trim it to the general shape of what you're trying to imitate it's a very good suggestive pattern of scuds, sowbugs, caddis pupae, caddis larvae and a variety of things like that. When I can I try to imitate a variety of things with one fly rather than one thing with one fly.

But I also get into exact imitations. Sometimes it's necessary, but I feel that exact imitation is overemphasized a lot in fly fishing literature. There are a lot of things that can trigger a fish into taking other than the exact thing they're feeding on at an exact time.

Q: What other patterns do you favor?
Tullis: The Thorax Dun is my basic dry-fly pattern. Color doesn't matter to me

88

so much as the wing silhouette, the shape and size.

I use Wiggle Bugs a lot in certain waters. They don't work very well where a lot of lures are used because the fish are already conditioned against that type of action by Rapalas, Flatfish, spinners and such. In fly-fishing-only waters they work extremely well. In the Henry's Fork, on Silver Creek and places like that, they work extremely well. And they don't classify as a lure anywhere; they're a hand-tied fly using traditional fly-tying materials and it's not molded to a hook. In Alaska they're super deadly on those big rainbow trout. The Wiggle Bug imitates almost exactly the swimming action of lamprey eels and leeches, and there are a lot of those in Alaska.

Glass Beads and *Daphnia* Clusters

Q: What other flies do you like?

Tullis: I use a lot of suggestive patterns. Buggy-looking nymphs, rubber legs for stones.

When I want to exactly imitate, with nymphs, I quite often go to a Skip Nymph, named by Skip Morris. It's kind of a combination between a Hare's Ear and a Pheasant Tail Nymph. But you can adapt the colors to make it look almost like the natural.

When it comes to bead heads I do something a little different. I go to glass-bead heads quite often so you can adapt the color to the color of the body and it still gives you the weight and sheen that you want. You don't get as much weight from glass as metal, but you get enough for small flies to do well.

I should mention that I use a lot of Mohair leeches in still water. And I imitate *Daphnia* clusters, which hardly anyone does.

Q: Daphnia clusters? What in the world are those?

Tullis: You don't know what *Daphnia* are? They're a small, almost microscopic crustacean, similar to a tiny shrimp or tiny scud. I figure where they're present in lakes in large numbers one third of the fish feed almost exclusively on *Daphnia*. Most people wouldn't ever catch those fish because they're feeding like whales do on plankton, go around with their mouths open. But I've discovered that if you get these multicolored Mohair yarns, wrap it on, put on a little marabou tail and brush it out, then to the fish it looks like a little cluster of these edibles and they'll come up and grab it. I'll even go so far as to put little dots of tee shirt paint on the fibers so it looks like the little dots of a cluster. The size of hook doesn't matter too much because you're not imitating a specific bug.

I've tied them as big as four inches long and the fish still eat them because they look like a big cluster, but most of the time I use a size 6 down to a size 10 hook. Just a fuzzy, non-descript kind of thing. Sometimes with a bead head and sometimes without. The bead head works as an attractor and keeps it level instead of riding hook-down. And I retrieve them very slow, say one inch a second, with long hesitations.

I've found through stomach pump samples that most of the fish I catch that way are full of the *Daphnia*. So I'm opening up the fishing in that lake to fish you wouldn't catch any other way. I'm convinced that they're taking the fly for clusters of *Daphnia*. It will also imitate a minnow if you fish it faster, or a damselfly nymph, or a dragonfly nymph or a leech. That's the kind of pattern I like, one that will imitate more than one thing.

Reviving Trout and Limiting the Catch

Q: Do you have any comments you want to make about environmental issues as they relate to the future of the sport?

Tullis: One thing that I've begun to get real involved with is proper catch-and-release. Teaching people how to play a fish quickly and how to release it gently.

Reviving a fish before releasing it is important, too. One thing Lefty Kreh taught me recently is to keep the fish's mouth open by holding onto his lower jaw while you're reviving him in the current. Another thing, I don't know how many people I've seen trying to revive a fish while they have their hand keeping the gill covers shut, thus keeping the water from flowing over the gills. That's just not helping the fish.

In addition to catch-and-release, it would be a good idea to limit the number of fish you catch. Even if you let them all go. Once you get into fly fishing you'll find there are certain days when you just have incredible numbers of fish. Many people don't realize, or don't want to realize, that there is a natural mortality rate no matter how gentle you are with fish. A certain number of caught fish will die because of stress or other factors. You've got to realize that fly fishing is a blood sport no matter how you want to look at it.

So if you're catching a lot of fish you might limit yourself by playing a little game. One of the games I like to play is "Two Fish Change Flies." Instead of sticking with the fly that you know is working, you've got to switch patterns with every two fish you catch. You learn a lot from that. That teaches you a lot with different patterns and how they work when fishing is good. It also limits the number of fish you catch. So you don't injure as many fish because you're not catching as many, but at the same time you're having fun because you're learning new things and experimenting.

One thing I notice is that people will go through stages in fly fishing, and "Two Fish Change Flies" is for a stage where you've already had days where you've caught lots of fish so you don't always need to go out and catch lots of them again just because you can. You can go out to the water and have fun, learn a few things and interact with the environment.

90

Stream-use Limitations

Q: How about stream-use limitations?

Tullis: I've found that fish adapt real well to heavy use if the regulations adapt along with it. If they let you keep fish, then the fish that you can keep will be gone. The Green River is a prime example. They let you keep one over 20 inches and two under 13 inches; as result, every fish is 13 to 20 inches. Very few bigger, very few smaller.

We've got to think of fishing differently than we used to. It's not a means of gathering food anymore, it's a means of sport and relaxation. And if we want to have it in the future we've got to make certain limitations now. I don't agree that every water should go catch-and-release. Some waters are family fisheries that are best suited to put-and-take fishing. You know, hatcheries dump a lot of fish in the lake and families come down, take home their limit, and I think that's fine. But if the river or lake is capable of growing trophy fish, then I think it should be managed as such. I think most people are headed in that direction.

Q: Is there anything that you want to add?

Tullis: Just that I think fly fishing should be well-rounded. There is such a variety of techniques and styles available that anybody can find something that suits them. Also, I think it's a mistake for a person to get so intent on technique that they forget about enjoying the overall fly fishing experience. Have fun.

Mike Lawson

Where to reach him:

Henry's Fork Anglers

H.C. 66, Box 491

Island Park, Idaho 83429

Phone: 208/558-7525

Professionally guides now: Very limited. "I don't do much guiding now. The shop has a staff of 15 guides, and I don't take request trips. But I like to get out enough to stay in touch with the actual guiding, so occasionally I'll just walk out of my office to handle the guiding when somebody books a trip."

Homewaters: "The Henry's Fork and its tributaries, but our shop does guiding on the Madison in Montana, and a bit in Yellowstone Park."

Born: 1946, Idaho Falls

Grew up: "I've spent my entire life in this part of Idaho."

Present fishing business affiliations: Henry's Fork Anglers, Island Park, Idaho

Publications and videos:

Videos: "Tying Western Dry Flies"(1986) and "Tying and Fishing Caddisflies" (1987), both produced by The Jack Dennis Fly Fishing Video Library.

Works in progress: Book, *Spring Creeks*; Video, "Tying and Fishing Spring Creek Patterns."

My interview with Mike Lawson was in his large study, a carefully finished basement room of his home in St. Anthony, Idaho. When I arrived at the appointed morning hour, he and his wife were entertaining another couple at breakfast. Rather than have me wait while they finished, Mike excused himself and we went downstairs to do our talking.

On the way to the lower level we passed a high-powered scope on a tripod, trained on a pothole toward the back of his sizable yard. Just then the pothole was occupied by a small flock of cinnamon teal.

In addition to a fax and other such office staples, one whole wall was devoted to bookcases holding a variety of books including Cadillac Desert, Reloading for Shotgunners *and a number of novels by such authors as Tom McGuane and Jeffrey Archer. Along another wall was a case holding enough rifles and shotguns that some would classify them as a collection.*

Mike Lawson is very serious about fly fishing and other things that matter. Mike's answers to my questions were direct, relatively succinct and a reflective pause—in the interest of accuracy—preceded most of them before delivery.

He was patient and unhurried, gracious about taking the better part of a half-day away from his business to talk to me. During our session he took several phone calls, but they were brief and businesslike. At one point I failed to press a button on the tape recorder and missed a few minutes of his answers; his response was to wave away my error as insignificant, and to go back patiently over the material I'd missed.

The ambiance of the interview was that I was in the presence of a man who understood that there is a right way and a wrong way to do most things, and that a big part of his satisfaction with life lay in doing things the right way. Put another way, he readily inspires confidence as both a man and as a fisherman.

Question: How did you happen to get into guiding, Mike?
Lawson: As a kid I learned to fish from my father and grandfather, and for me it was always fly fishing. I've never owned a spinning rod in my life. Fly fishing was always a part of my life, but I'd never considered doing any guiding until about 1971, after I was out of college.

When I was a student at Brigham Young I lived up in Island Park, Idaho, in the summers and worked for the Forest Service, and that's how I got started learning the Henry's Fork. Then one day, after college, I was fishing on the river and Jim Danskin asked me if I'd be interested in guiding. I said yes and it sort of went from there. Actually, Danskin hired me because I knew the Henry's Fork, but it turned out that most of my early guiding was on the Madison.

Guiding Is Teaching

Q: What attitudes do people bring to a guided fishing trip that affect their enjoyment of the experience?

Lawson: I think the biggest problem is a client expecting too much. Hiring a guide is expensive, so I don't blame people for feeling that they need to get a real good day for their money. And that's what we try to do. But as far as basing the success of a trip on the number of fish caught, that's a mistake. I'll have people ask at the beginning of the day, "How many fish are we going to catch today?" I don't know the answer to that any more than I know how many I'm going to catch when I go fishing.

Or they'll say, "I want to catch a six-pound trout today." That's just not a reasonable expectation. I might fish all summer and not catch a six-pound trout myself.

A person is better off if he has the attitude of learning some things from the guide that will make him a better fisherman in the future.

Q: So, when guiding, you consider yourself a teacher?

Lawson: Oh, yes, there really is a lot of teaching in guiding. My favorite kind of client is one who is interested in learning as well as having fun, rather than just being concerned with the result—the number and size of fish they catch.

Frankly, that's the way most of the customers are, they want to learn some things and have fun.

Why Hire a Guide?

Q: When should a person hire a guide to go fishing?

Lawson: There are really three basic reasons to hire a guide. The first is to learn fly fishing technique, whether the client is a beginner or more advanced. A guide can teach that.

The second reason is to learn the area. To learn where the good fishing places in the area are, and how to get access to them. The idea that guides don't want to show people good places to fish is generally wrong.

The third reason to hire a guide is simple recreation and convenience. Like someone who wants to float a river and hires a guide mostly because the guide has the boat and other equipment to do that, and the guide can row the boat.

As for people hiring a guide in order to improve their fishing techniques, we have one client who comes all the way from Japan every year to fish with us, and he only wants to fish the Harriman State Park area of the Henry's Fork. That's one of the most demanding fisheries in the world, and even the best fishermen don't catch much there. But this particular client doesn't care if he catches a fish. He comes to learn and to improve his technique and he says he learns more from a day on that part of the Henry's Fork than he does fishing anywhere else.

As for the second reason to hire a guide, to learn about the fishing in an area, I think that when somebody goes into an area to fish for the first time he needs to hire a guide. You can learn more about the fishing there in one day than you could learn in weeks on your own. When I go to a new area I like to hire a guide, at least for the first day, and I want to ask him questions about access and such things, and if he doesn't want to share that information with me then I really don't feel like he's doing his job. If he's trying to protect his waters just for clients he's guiding, I believe that's wrong.

Expensive Versus Cheap Tackle

Q: In your experience as a guide, what mistakes do clients make in tackle and equipment selection? Are there things they spend too much or too little on?

Lawson: The most common mistake is just having cheap junk tackle. It's really hard to learn from that kind of stuff. People sometimes think of trout fishing as an elitist, expensive sport, but when you compare the total dollar outlay to other sports—like golf or skiing—then I think fishing is a relatively inexpensive sport. The equipment is going to be a lifetime investment and I think it's a mistake to go down and buy it at K-Mart. Primarily, I'm speaking of rods.

Most people come pretty well equipped as far as tackle is concerned. But often they come unprepared for the elements. Especially cold weather. You know most people from out of this area don't realize that it can snow in July. And a 40 degree day in July feels a lot colder than a 40 degree day in April.

Click Drag Is More Than Adequate

Q: How do you feel about reels that people show up with? Is there some overkill there sometimes?

Lawson: Sometimes people show up with a super expensive fly reel with a disc drag and all that, and they'll have spent $500 on it. That's overkill, but it's going to do the job. A reel like that will handle everything from light trout to big strong fish. But it's something you really don't need.

Q: How do you feel about disc drag versus click drag? Is a disc drag worth the extra money?

Lawson: For most of the trout fishing we do, a click drag is more than adequate.

Q: Any other items of equipment that you want to mention?

Lawson: Yes, nets. That's an area where you don't want to skimp on price. For catch-and-release these cheap nets with the green nylon mesh are terrible. They really tear a fish up. The roughness of them peels scales and slime off the fish. The net needs to have a real soft net bag and those are more expensive.

95

Mistakes of Average Fishermen

Q: In your guiding experience, what common errors in fishing technique does the average fisherman make?

Lawson: One of the most common mistakes is too much false casting. They have the line in the air too much. If they're floating they're not really covering the water. If they're wade-fishing, the unnecessary false casting, flashing the line over the fish, increases the chance of spooking those fish. I think most fishermen don't get as close to the fish as they should. They try to cast too much line and that requires false casting. Any of us can cast more accurately at 20 feet than we can at 50. We can make a 20-foot cast without false casting; with a 50-foot cast, usually we can't.

In order to get within 20 feet of a trout you've got to be able to do it without spooking him. So we work hard at teaching people how to stalk and approach fish. That's really important.

Q: What other mistakes does the average fisherman make?

Lawson: In addition to too much false casting and staying too far from the fish, a lot of people have a tendency to rip the line back off the water. Especially if they don't make the right cast. Instead of fishing the drift out so it's well beyond the fish, they'll just yank it off the water, make a big disturbance and put the fish down.

Learn About Trout

Q: If there were a few rules or suggestions that you'd give the average fisherman to help them improve their non-guided fishing, what would they be?

Lawson: People, in general, need to learn more about trout. And that's not just beginners. They need to do more reading about trout and what kind of creatures they really are. How they see, how they hear, how they sense danger, how they find their food and where they live.

We teach clients that a trout has three basic requirements for survival. The first is protection from his enemies. The second is the need to rest from the current; they can't fight the current all the time. The third thing is the availability of food.

They're going to hold a position in the stream that offers the most of those requirements. A trout doesn't always manage to get all of them. For example, the place that offers protection from enemies may not offer a very good food opportunity, so they'll feed near the areas where there's some protection.

How Trout See

Q: You mentioned the value of knowing how trout see. Why is that important?

Lawson: Knowing how a trout sees relates to how and why we can get close to a fish. And we have to impress that on people.

Trout have very good close-up focus. We can put our finger on the end of our nose and can't focus on it, but a trout's eyes could. And what they sacrifice for the ability to focus close up is that they can't focus on infinity like we can; they can focus on it but they can only see an unclear background.

Another thing, when trout feed they focus their eyes on the food. Even though they could probably see you if they changed their focus, they don't change it while they're feeding. So when trout are feeding, if you're careful, you can walk right up on them.

And knowing such things about trout has as much to do with fishing success as does knowing where to fish.

Stream Etiquette

Q: What other rules would you pass along?

Lawson: It's more for beginners than for experienced fishermen, but I think they need to understand some basic rules of conduct and etiquette on the stream. They need to learn to share the water. We teach people to walk around other fishermen and to try to determine what water the other fisherman is fishing. For instance, if you're on a small stream and the other fisherman is fishing upstream, you don't want to just move up to the next pool in front of him. You need to give him plenty of water to fish.

Landing Fish

Q: What do you teach clients about landing fish?

Lawson: Most people pretty much let the fish play them rather than playing the fish. The main thing you want to do in playing a fish is to disorient him, and the best way to do that is to determine which direction the fish is going, then to put pressure in the opposite direction. If he starts to swim to his right, you want to immediately bend the rod down to the left.

When you're playing a fish don't point the rod straight up, like the Orvis position. You want to use that only if the fish is running straight away from you. You use it then because the higher you can hold the rod the more line you can keep out of the water, and the less drag there's going to be.

When the fish is going to the side, though, you want to keep him disoriented and also you want to be finding a good place for yourself to be when you actually land the fish. If you're standing out in the swift current and you're trying to drag that fish through it, it's tough. I tell people to try to get to the bank. You can get more side pressure on a fish when you're on the bank, and also there is usually quiet water there. If you can't get to the bank then at least get into the lee of a rock or something where there's not so much current.

Short Casts More Important Than Long

Q: Moving on from what you teach clients to your own personal fishing techniques, how important are long casts?

Lawson: I cast long distances to fish only when I can't wade close to the fish. Being able to make a long cast is important, but maybe not for the distance; with wind you've got to have the ability to drive the fly into it, to know how to develop additional line speed. So practicing long casting is good.

But I think a lot of us don't spend enough time practicing the short, accurate cast. And I'm a firm believer that every cast you make to a fish after the first cast diminishes your chances of catching that fish. There are exceptions, but I think you have to approach a fish with that attitude.

So I like to get close. I like to stalk the fish. Part of the fun I have in fishing is observing a feeding fish and trying to stalk fairly close to the fish and not making a lot of false casts.

Q: You said that there are exceptions to your generalization that your first cast is the best chance to catch the fish. What are some of those exceptions?

Lawson: There are times, like on the Henry's Fork, when there are so many bugs on the water that fish get into a feeding rhythm. You see a trout rising and he takes one bug and lets 40 bugs float over him. Being naturals, it's like every one of those 40 is a perfect imitation. The fact is that there are just too many on the water for him to eat every one, and it may take dozens of casts to get the fly at the right place at the right moment.

It isn't that the fly is wrong, but I notice when I'm guiding fishermen at a time like that, they start wanting to change flies. They get a good drift over the fish and can't understand why the fish didn't take their fly. Fact is, you might have to make a lot of casts to that fish, and the more accurate drifts you can get over him the better your chances are of being there at just the right time.

So the idea that every cast diminishes your chances doesn't apply in that situation. And you should be close enough that you're not having to false cast. You should cast, drift over the fish, cast again and drift again—then every cast is a fishing cast. But if you're standing way back you have to false cast, and your accuracy is going to be off.

Learning From Spooky Fish Down Under

Q: How do your own personal fishing techniques differ from those of other good fishermen?

Lawson: I think that one of the biggest influences on my fishing was taking a few trips to New Zealand. Those fish are extremely wary, the water is crystal clear and they're not accustomed to seeing a lot of fishermen.

The slightest movement will send those New Zealand fish running for cover. That can be a crunching of gravel, the fish seeing the fly-line flash into his window of vision or making a noise by stepping on a rock wrong. It's almost all sight-fishing where you see the fish in the water before you go after him.

Every trip I've learned things that I can utilize at home. Like how to stalk fish and actually learning to see fish in the water even if they're not feeding. I like to use that same technique now on most of the trout streams I fish. I use it a lot when I fish the Beaverhead. I like to kind of work up the bank, and if you're careful you can see those fish in their holding positions. And if you know where the fish is, then you've got an advantage in knowing where to make your cast without spooking him.

The Fisherman As Hunter

Q: I'm sitting across the room from a guncase full of rifles and shotguns, and I'm aware that even though you're talking fishing, you sound like a hunter. Do you think there's some similarity in the two sports?

Lawson: There sure is a similarity. That hunting attitude is part of what I was saying about just staying on the bank of a trout stream and observing.

For instance, one of the birds that is the most intriguing to me is the great blue heron. Just watch those birds. They rely totally on stealth to catch their food. They have to be able to stalk a fish because they only can walk in a stream or a lake to fish; they can't dive down on the fish from out of the air. I know they have to get close enough that the fish can see them. So they've got to move slow enough that the fish doesn't realize the bird is there. Then they'll wait until just the right time, and when they make their attack it's fast and accurate. I think we need to incorporate some of those great blue heron skills in our fishing.

Importance of Good Position

Q: What other things do you do in your personal fishing that are different?

Lawson: One thing I do that I think a lot of other fishermen don't do is to change position. Like they'll be in a spot where they're having trouble getting a good drag-free drift over a fish and they'll put on longer leaders and smaller diameter tippets and try to mend more line. And a lot of time just moving yourself a few feet lets you get an easy drag-free drift. Maybe it's going to take more than a few feet. Maybe if you're fishing across and can't get a good drift you'll have to back out and get straight below the fish. So I think you've got to have the willingness to move around.

Small Selection of Fly Patterns

Q: Are you the kind of fisherman who uses a wide variety of patterns or do you use just a few favorite ones?

WISDOM OF THE GUIDES

Lawson: Usually, I just use a small selection of patterns. I always carry an Adams, and I especially like a Parachute Adams. I like Humpies, Royal Wulffs and Elk Hair Caddis'. Those are my basic patterns. Also, I like terrestrials, such as ants and beetles.

When I fish the water I'm most familiar with, which would be the Henry's Fork, then I generally know what bugs are going to be on the water so I take patterns that are appropriate, like taking Pale Morning Duns if I know that's what's on the river. So when I'm fishing real familiar water I'm more into the match-the-hatch kind of thinking. But just for general all-around fishing I follow the rule of bigger flies early in the season and smaller flies later, and I don't get overwhelmed with too many patterns.

The main thing to remember about fly selection is that the size of the fly is a lot more important than the specific pattern. It's a general rule on a lot of trout streams that the biggest insects come out earliest in the year, with the exception of real early, like in March and April when we have little *Baetis* flies.

Early in the year I'm going to carry my basic flies in size 10 and 12s and the smallest I'd be using would be 16s. But in August I'd probably move the 10s and 12s clear out of my box; that time of year, no matter what river you fish, the insects are usually small.

Q: You're talking dry flies. How about nymphs?
Lawson: I much prefer dry-fly fishing to nymphs, and when I do fish nymphs I just don't feel that nymph patterns are as critical as when fishing on the surface. Except during the emergence of some particular insect, fish are offered a wide variety of food types when they're feeding underwater and so I don't feel like I have to be very specific in patterns. I'll use a Prince Nymph or a Pheasant Tail Nymph most of the time unless I'm fishing a big river where there might be stonefly nymphs, and then I use a simple black Rubber-legs. I don't fish a wide variety of nymph patterns.

Q: How about streamers and soft hackles?
Lawson: I don't do as much streamer fishing as dry fly, but I do quite a bit. When I was young, soft hackles were mostly what we used. They were wet flies, all soft-hackle patterns, and we'd usually fish two or three of them at once. Just swing them in the current. They still work real well.

Mike As Fly Designer

Q: You've designed some fly patterns, haven't you?
Lawson: Yes, over the years I've developed a lot of flies because this river can be pretty demanding. They're all flies that have come about from need, rather than just sitting down and thinking up some wild pattern.

The Henry's Fork Hopper is one of my patterns. I started tying that in 1972 before we had our shop. Even though there are now probably 200 different hopper patterns, back then there were only about four of them. And up here on the Henry's Fork only one of those patterns worked; a quill body pattern described by Vince Marinaro for the Letort River. It wasn't the Letort Hopper. That's one that doesn't work for this river. But Marinaro's pattern was very complex. I tied some and they were really involved. So I decided to use his philosophy, but I substituted elk hair for quill, for the body, did some other little different things with it and came up with the Henry's Fork Hopper. We've never had any reason to change it, and it's still one of our top patterns.

The Importance of Being Ernest's Son

Q: Isn't the Hemingway Caddis one of your designs? Is that pattern named for Ernest Hemingway?

Lawson: That was kind of a combination of mine and my friend René Harrop. He's a neighbor and, by the way, I consider him to be the finest fly tier in the country. A lot of what I've learned I originally learned from René. The Hemingway was originally a modification of the Henryville into different colors for a fly shop in Michigan. Then we started tying them in a medium dun color to match the hatches we get here in the spring, and we changed the design of the fly a little bit. At the time Jack Hemingway, Ernest Hemingway's son, was doing a lot of fishing over here, and René started tying some of those dun-colored flies for Jack. When we opened our shop we wanted to carry that fly, but we'd never given it a name. It had kind of become Jack's favorite, so we named it the Hemingway Caddis.

Q: Some people insist on using natural materials in flies. They rebel against using synthetics. How do you feel on that subject?

Lawson: I like to use natural materials more than synthetics, and I do it when I can. But sometimes synthetics are really fine. Like Antron for dubbing and for Gary LaFontaine's caddis patterns. There are natural materials that will incorporate a lot of that, but they're almost impossible to get anymore. Such as seal fur. It had some excellent qualities of shine and brightness. It's the same with polar bear hair.

The Madison and Whirling Disease

Q: A while back you mentioned the Madison River. What's your reaction to what's going on there, and elsewhere, with whirling disease?

Lawson: I think whirling disease has taken a real toll on the Madison. I'm not inclined to dispute the research that's been done over there. We find in our own guiding that the number of rainbows there has really dropped off compared to five or six years ago.

I think whirling disease is the biggest piece of the puzzle, but I think there are other things. The tremendous fishing pressure has had some impact, and I think some very erratic stream flow management has been very detrimental to the rainbow trout in their spawning.

I think there isn't the success in spawning in the Madison that there was 11 or 12 years ago because in that time the river has been so high it's almost washed the highway out. It just comes ripping down in May and early June and changes whole channels of the river. There are channels that used to have water that are dry now. And there used to be tremendous numbers of trout spawning in those dried-up channels.

What I'm saying is, if there were three times the number of juvenile trout as there are now, then maybe whirling disease wouldn't have as much of an impact. But I don't know that, it's just a feeling I have. Whirling disease seems so prevalent over there, but there must be a certain percentage of juvenile trout that have some sort of genetic resistance to it, and I feel that if there were more juvenile fish then there would be more trout that are resistant to it.

I really congratulate Montana for what they're doing there. I think they're prepared to do whatever is necessary, including closing the whole river to fishing. But I think this thing will run its course if left alone because there is a certain percentage of fish that are genetically resistant. Maybe only ten percent of the juveniles survived when whirling disease killed 90 percent of the trout. Well, this ten percent, when they spawn, will probably produce offspring of which 50 percent will be of a resistant strain. And gradually, that percentage of resistant trout will increase back to where things are normal. So I think now is the time to really focus on protecting these fish and seeing that everything is done so that they can have an optimal survival of their young-of-the-year fish.

I think that's going to take some stream-flow adjustments. They've got to start running more water earlier in the year so we don't have these big blowouts. It's got to have some effect on spawning success. It just has to. There are some tailwater rivers that have no spawning success just because of that one thing. They just run so much water at certain times that the young trout just get washed out. One of those rivers has been the Green River in Utah.

One thing trout need is relatively stable stream flow during spawning. That's why they like to spawn in spring-fed streams so much. If there's a spring creek that enters a river it will be loaded with trout in the spring. Or in the fall if they're brown trout.

That's why I say that when a river has problems, it's usually not due to just one thing alone. It's a complex issue most of the time when you have problems with fisheries.

102

In my opinion, in Colorado they're always going to have problems with whirling disease because they just continue to stock fish, and those fish are just new hosts for whirling disease to have available to them. The fish they're stocking haven't had a chance to develop any resistance to the disease, and they never will. I think they rely on stocked fish more than any other state in the West.

Catch-and-Release

Q: How do you feel about catch-and-release?

Lawson: I think it's a good thing, but I don't think we can impose it on all fishermen. The heritage of a lot of our local residents is to catch fish and bring some home to eat. That's one place where I believe I may have an advantage over some other people in my business in that I've lived here all my life so I know how these people think. You just can't push 'em too far because when you do they react, and sometimes you can lose what you have.

If it were just up to me, and I didn't have to worry about how other people felt about it, I'd probably have everything be catch-and-release. But you have to be careful about pushing people around too much.

You've got to educate people to the benefits of catch-and-release and just move slow. But I do think catch-and-release is the only real answer to fishing pressure and crowds, either total or in modified form. Another thing that does help a lot though is slot limits.

Q: Any last thoughts for us, words of wisdom?

Lawson: I think a big thing for fishermen is to just learn to enjoy their time on the river rather than concentrating on the fishing so much.

Take 10 or 15 minutes out of every hour's fishing and sit on the bank. Look at the water. You can learn a lot by just watching the river and watching other people fish, see if you can see what they're doing right and what they're doing wrong. And enjoy yourself.

We all get a little too focused on the fishing sometimes and miss some of the real nice things that fly fishing has to offer. If you just spend eight hours a day looking at your fly on the water you miss a lot of things—like an osprey diving into the river to catch a fish, some deer on the bank or maybe some songbirds in the bushes. I think people need to learn to relax and not approach fishing like it's a matter of life or death.

Charlie Gilman

How to reach him:

> 2690 O Road
>
> Hotchkiss, Colorado 81419
>
> Phone & fax: 970/835-3658
>
> USA phone: 800/653-0096

Professionally guides now: Yes

Homewaters: Gunnison River,
Taylor River and Dolores River, all in Colorado. Also licensed in Montana. Has guided in upstate New York, Alaska, New Zealand (since 1986), Russia, Costa Rica, Argentina, Chile and Mexico.

Born: 1951 in Ponca City, Oklahoma. Grew up in Colorado and Oklahoma (third generation mining family from Colorado). Learned to fly fish on the Colorado streams he now guides.

Guiding history: Has been guiding since 1985 for trout.

Present fishing business affiliations:

> Colorado: Western Anglers at Crested Butte, Gunnison Pleasure Park
> at the confluence of the Black Canyon of the Gunnison;
>
> Montana: Hatch Finders Guide Service in Livingston;
>
> International: International Fly Fisher (Worldwide Fly Fishing
> Adventures), Hotchkiss, Colorado; Fly Fish Kola, Sweden.

Charlie Gilman and I talked fishing on a patio behind his house in rural Hotchkiss, Colorado. Actually, the patio was part of the guest quarters that Charlie maintains for his clients. In addition to housing clients on the premises, Charlie and his family also raise pheasants. The entire spread had the feel of being controlled by folks who prefer to go first class and know how to do it.

Charlie and I sat at an umbrella table on that patio for the better part of a fine September morning. The conversation was intermittently interrupted by a couple of fellows asking Charlie's advice and instructions on work being done about the place. Certainly there is nothing pretentious, and no hint of arrogance, about Charlie, but the ambiance of the interview somehow had a baronial feel, as if I were talking to a convivial and casually dressed Lord of the Manor.

We started with coffee and ended with lemonade. The time went quickly because of Charlie's fast wit and ready laugh. After I folded the recording equipment away we made the 15-minute drive down to the Gunnison River. There had been rain and the water was up and off-color. But Charlie wanted to see if he couldn't catch some trout for photographs.

He nymphed upstream, using two white pinch-on indicators as he had described in his interview. He got a good fish on for a moment, but our conversation and picture-taking distracted him enough that he missed a solid hookup. A few casts later he hooked a 14-inch rainbow, which I photographed. Then, for an encore, he caught another one of about the same size. He was in the water a total of about 20 minutes and had pretty much stood in the same spot, about 20 feet from the bank and 40 feet from his truck. It all looked so easy, like anyone could have done it.

As we were leaving he apologized that conditions were so bad, that he hadn't been able to produce better for the pictures.

Question: *When you take clients out fishing what do you consider your role as a guide?*
Gilman: I always take them to the fish. I think 90 percent of a guide's job is to take the clients to the fish, give them some recommendations on patterns and give them some recommendations on presentation. The rest of the job depends on how well the client listens or how far along their ability is.

But my major thing I want to instill in anyone is not how well they did that day, but did they leave with a little piece of knowledge so when they're on their own it's going to make them a better fisherman.

Then I start letting a few tricks out. We've all got a few little tricks in our bag. You know that. And as people progress you show them more.

Charlie and His Clients

Q: How do you feel about clients who've never held a fly rod before?

Gilman: I love beginners because they've got the most open mind. For instance up in Montana, around Dillon, I start people out on knots, then I put them in a float tube in the Clark Canyon Reservoir with the proper leader and the proper fly. They learn how to mend their line and how to kick the tube around, then they learn how to play fish. Big fish. And that's a good start because that gets them hooked on the sport. Then you take them to the Beaverhead, and you say, "Now you've got to learn how to do it." By then, they have motivation.

Q: What kind of clients do you generally prefer to guide?

Gilman: My favorite kind of client is a client with a good attitude. By that I mean someone who's willing to learn something new, who doesn't think that because they paid a guide fee they bought fish, and who realize that they have to have some ability to catch fish.

Q: How would you describe your least favorite kind of client?

Gilman: My least favorite kind of client would be a person who has high expectations of catching fish even though they don't have much skill. Another kind is the person who expects to be pampered, who should have hired a valet instead of a guide.

Fishing Too Close

Q: What common shortcomings, as fishermen, do you find in your clients?

Gilman: In the West, people generally tend to fish with too short of a rod and cast too short of a line. They try to get too close to the fish, right up on top of them.

For a wild trout, I don't like to get any closer than 30 feet. Of course, we have streams in the West where you can get right on top of the fish, like the Green, and it just ruins you for when you go to a wild river somewhere and actually have to catch a smart fish. Fish get tame like that because they've been caught-and-released so much they know what's going on. And that's happening in every river in Colorado where they have catch-and-release. Basically, it's a tailwater phenomenon.

Stay Out of the Water

Q: Can you list a few rules for people to improve their fishing?

Gilman: First, stay out of the water when at all possible. That's a hard one, because everybody wants to get in that water and wade around. I take them up to Red Rock Creek, that tiny, beautiful Montana spring creek, and they've got to stand in that damned water.

106

Q: Why should they stay out of the water?
Gilman: Because of the shock waves you send out when you step in the water. One step into the water can send shock waves out about 40 feet into the pool, even though you don't see it. So you stay out of the water to keep from notifying the fish that you're there. Which is a big start, isn't it? Because if the fish know that you're there, I don't care how good you can cast, I don't care what pattern you have, you've got problems.

Importance of Correct Leaders

Q: What other rules?
Gilman: Rule two, your terminal tackle is probably 50 percent of your success. By that I mean the length, the size and configuration of your leader.

Of course, your terminal tackle depends on the conditions. The situation dictates. I spend more time lengthening and shortening leaders than I do fishing, especially with nymph fishing. Trying to get the drift I want at the depth I want. But the length, size and configuration of your leader is important with dry flies, as well.

Number three, most people are very sloppy knot tiers. They need to use more knots and they need to learn to tie them properly.

Q: You mentioned the lengthening and shortening of leaders. Why might you shorten a leader?
Gilman: If you're nymphing in a situation where the fish are in fast, shallow water you've got to shorten your leader or you won't detect the strikes. Or maybe if you are hanging-up on bottom rocks because the leader's too long.

Maybe I should mention here that for nymphing, just for nymphing, I use a level leader for the full length of the leader. And I use limp leader material for that, in 3X or 4X. By limp leader material I mean Tectan, Orvis or Rio.

I use just a level leader because there is less resistance on that line so the line tends to hang more straight down in the water.

Q: Do you do that in shallow water too, like two or three feet deep?
Gilman: Absolutely. Because the trouble with the tapered leaders is that you have a belly in your leader so you're detecting the strike way too late. And that's true whether you're fishing deep or shallow. If you're using something heavy and stiff, like Maxima, it tends to go horizontal in the water, and that's why you're using the thin, flexible type leader, to get away from that.

Dry-Fly Leaders

Q: How about dry-fly leaders?
Gilman: I go up to 20 feet on a dry-fly leader. My favorite length, for ability

cast and all, is about 14 to 15 feet, with about four feet of that being tippet. And hand-tied. I hate manufactured leaders.

I use 12-pound-test for the butt section of my dry-fly leaders, and in Maxima that's about 1X. Manufacturers, and most people, use a 30- or 40-pound butt. So my terminal tackle is way different. I use the light-weight leader for two reasons, line splash and visibility. A butt section is way more visible than a fly line when it's 30-pound-test, and it hits the water like a ton of bricks.

And if you're trying to catch big fish in shallow water, you just can't do it with a heavy butt section. Why use a three-weight line and then put a piece of 30-pound-test right out there in front of your fly? It doesn't make any sense. Whatever size line you're using, your leader should have less splash than the line. It's just that simple.

People say that you need a heavy butt section to make the leader turn over. But I get the leader to turn over and I do it with minimum line splash. So I'm not really making any casting compromise by using the light leader and light butt section. Actually, in high wind it will cast better.

For someone who's not used to it, a leader like that might require a little better timing in their casting.

Tapering Leaders

Q: What principles do you follow in tapering your dry-fly leaders?
Gilman: The specific formula each time has to meet the conditions of the stream. I can't sit here and say use three feet of this diameter and three feet of that diameter.

The leader can have a slight belly in it, like a fly line. If I'm fishing in ideal conditions it will be a direct taper down. I'd go from 12-pound Maxima to, say, 8-pound Tectan down to 5-pound Tectan. Then either that will be the tippet or I'll put one more piece on in addition to that.

But if I'm in a heavy wind situation I'll go from the 12-pound Maxima to 12-pound Tectan. Same strength, but different type of material with just a little bit more weight in the middle of the leader. So that gives me some belly, just like your fly line belly; in both cases the belly helps to get it out. Now it's got to be at least a 20-mile-an-hour wind before I'll resort to that. But from 20- to 40-mile-an-hour winds, that's what you've got to do. And we fish in 20- to 40-mile-an-hour winds all the time.

I remember one windy day I was fishing with Dick Talleur and he refused to fish in such conditions and went back to the van. Pretty soon he came back to the water and said that he was afraid the van was going to blow over so he decided to go back to fishing for his own safety. That was a day we caught 12 fish over eight pounds.

Knots

Q: In an earlier answer you were critical of the average fisherman's knots. What knots do you commonly use?

Gilman: I use a nail knot from fly line to leader. I use a blood knot to make a leader and I use a double blood knot when I'm tying two different types or sizes of materials together. Like connecting hard material to soft material. So what you do on the light side of the tippet you double your line, so then they pull down the same.

Q: Why do you use a blood knot instead of a double surgeon's knot?

Gilman: Personally, I just don't get as much strength from a surgeon's knot. Some people can get by with a surgeon's knot, but I like a blood knot better.

Q: What knot do you use to connect the fly?

Gilman: I really prefer loop knots on my flies, especially with wet flies and especially in lake fishing. I use a Duncan loop. The reason you use any loop is so the fly can hinge off the end of the line and have action. I use the Duncan loop because it slips, and that acts as a shock absorber. When those big fish hit in the lake you need just a little bit of give so you don't snap the leader off on the strike.

Sighting Fish

Q: Are there any other rules you'd have folks follow to catch more fish?

Gilman: I'd say the next thing is learning to read the water and to look for fish before you fish. Those are both important. If you can see where the fish are without entering the water, then you've already got the upper hand on them.

One of the first things I teach everywhere is that you want to look and know where all your fish are. And you might have to fish to get to your fish. For instance, say you see a nice fish and cast directly to him and line another, closer fish and scare him away, then he's going to screw up the whole pool. Spook one, spook them all. He's going to run and scare all the other fish off.

Learning how to sight fish is very important. There's a knack to it, and most people don't yet have it. And once you sight a fish, then you can tell if it's a feeding fish or a non-feeding fish. There's no point fishing for a non-feeding fish. If a fish is on the bottom, not suspended, and if he's not going from side to side then he's not feeding. If he's suspended in the water or if you see a slight sideways movement then you've got a feeding fish. You can tell whether or not he's suspended by whether or not he has a shadow.

Q: You wouldn't try to catch a non-feeding fish?

Gilman: Well, if it's really a slow day and there's just nothing going on, then you might try to force feed one. But generally, it will blow up in your face.

The Trout's Window of Vision

Q: Any other rules for catching fish?

Gilman: The last thing is presentation and line control. If you know where a fish is you need to know what that fish sees, his window and his periphery of vision. You want to put the fly not right in his window, but to one side of his window.

Q: Why do you want the fly outside of his window?

Gilman: You just want to distract him. You don't want to put a fly where he can read the brand of the hook. You want him to catch sight of the fly out of the corner of his eye. Then, the next thing is that he's heard it hit and he sees it out of the corner of his eye, so now he's more worried about it getting away. It probably hasn't occurred to him yet that it might be an imitation. Because he's not spooked and he's feeding.

So more times than not, in that kind of situation, he'll rush over and take the fly because he hasn't had time to look it over.

Line Control

Q: And how about line control?

Gilman: Line control is the last thing people learn. And it's one of the most important things. At first when you're teaching someone you want to show them how to get a good dead drift and of course, to keep it simple, you do that by using a real slack line. Then about the last thing is to teach them how to control their line so that they're getting that dead drift with the line just slack enough to do the job, so that they're that close to having a tight line.

I'd say line control is probably the biggest thing that people need to work on. And the mistake they make is over-mending. Most people mend way too often. They don't know why they're doing it, they just know they're supposed to do it.

When you're fishing big fish, or spooky fish, you have to put the mend in the line when you cast, so that when it hits the water the mend's already in it. Then afterwards, if you have to and it's a long run, then one mend is allowed. But a lot of times I get people who, I swear, must mend the line 50 times in one cast. There's a froth in the water. You want to say, "My God, you sure can mend line!" They do it because they want you to know that they know how to mend the line.

I take people to New Zealand who don't know how to mend line—never heard of it—and I don't tell them about it. They don't spend the day slapping the water and consequently they'll end up with more fish at the end of the day than the quote expert that's mending his line all day and wondering what's gone wrong.

The other thing I just hate is what some people do after making a bad cast. There's no such thing as a "bad cast" in my book. You always play it out. Sometimes when people make a cast they don't like, they rip the line right back off the water and say, "Let's try it again." They want the guide to see how good they can really cast, so they put the fly right back there with a better cast, and say, "How's that one?" I say, "That would have been great if that was your first cast. But the fish is gone now."

Q: What should people do when they make a bad cast?

Gilman: When they make a bad cast they should fish it out, no matter where it ends up. They should let it drift past the area that's being fished, then gently get it back in. Because making a disturbance raising the line off the water is as bad as mending too much. The problem is one of attitude, like, "Oh, no, dammit. That's not my best cast." But the best cast doesn't always get the fish. I've caught them behind me before. Attitude is everything. Patience and attitude.

Mend Casts

Q: You mentioned mending the line in the air. How do you manage that?

Gilman: For dry-fly fishing I like oval casts a lot. Joan and Lee Wulff developed the oval cast. It's a side cast that has an oval in it, and when you put the fly on the water the mend is there. With an oval cast you've usually got enough for a whole drift. Other than an oval cast, learning how to do a regular slack cast is important. That's where you overpower your cast and then bring it back to you just a little bit so it settles down into a nice little 'S' curve.

Those two casts are the most important ones to know, as far as I'm concerned. There's a lot better casters than I am who can do all sorts of trick casts, like Spey casting. The last thing you want to do, though, is start slapping the water with that line once it's on the water. You want the mend built into the cast. Absolutely. No doubt about it.

Distance Casting

Q: How important is distance in casting?

Gilman: The main thing about casting that gets to me with beginners is they think that a shorter line is easier to cast. It's not. You have to have enough line out so that the belly of the line will load your rod properly. If you're casting and still have the belly of the line on the reel then you're not going to be able to load your rod.

I had this guy who weighed about 200 pounds and he had about ten feet of line out. I watched him using his whole body, working to get his casts out. I told him to put about 20 more feet of line out and you won't have to do that; the rod will do the work for you.

Fly Patterns

Q: For your personal fishing do you like to carry a lot of fly patterns or just a few?

Gilman: Within the truck somewhere I always have about 10,000 flies. On my person I pick out one small fly box with about three to six of my favorite patterns for dries, nymphs and streamers. I've got a bunch of those boxes and each one is going to have some Royal Wulffs, some Green Drakes, some Au Sable Wulffs, some Black Caddis', some Compara-duns, and up in Montana, some Elk Hair Caddis'.

In my personal fishing, at the end of a season's fishing, I'll have used maybe only five patterns of dries and five patterns of nymphs. It changes from year to year, but right now the dries are pretty much the ones I just mentioned.

Q: How about nymphs?

Gilman: As for nymphs, a Callibaetis Flashback is a good generic, attractor fly so there's always a bunch of those in my box. I've always got some Pheasant Tail Nymphs in my box, both in natural and in olive. I always have some soft hackles like a Red-Ass Kelso for when things get tough. Any soft hackle with a peacock body and a partridge hackle.

Q: And streamers?

Gilman: I basically fish a grizzly marabou Woolly Bugger pattern. In New Zealand it's called a Cockabully, which is also what they call a sculpin down there. The tail and hackle are grizzly and the body is a dubbing I make out of a mixture of purple, black and brown Antron dubbing. And I use an olive Woolly Bugger.

And that's about it. If I can't catch fish on any of those flies, then they're just not biting.

Selecting a Rod

Q: What mistakes do people make in what they spend for equipment?

Gilman: They make mistakes both in spending too much and in spending too little. But I'd rather have them overequipped than underequipped. Beginners, especially, should have more expensive tackle, particularly a good rod.

People don't generally appreciate, I think, how much difference a good rod makes. Last year in New Zealand I fished with a friend of mine and he broke all his good rods the first week we were there.

So, with a week of fishing still to go, what he had left was a Shakespeare graphite composite, about a twenty-dollar fly rod. He said, "I can fish with this. It looks just like those other rods." And he was ready to quit fly fishing at the end of the day.

112

He says, "I can't cast. What's the matter with me?" I told him to go back and get one of my Loomis rods. He started using the Loomis and said, "I can cast!"

So the rod really does make a difference.

Selecting a Reel

Q: How about reels?

Gilman: Reels are a different thing. See, I'm a Loop reel distributor so I'm sold on Loops. But let's face it, there are a lot of reels that are adequate, especially for beginners. Once you get into playing large fish and have to feed them a lot of line and keep a constant tension on them, then the larger diameter reels give you a great advantage because the line comes off smoother and in bigger loops.

Q: I've heard people tout those large diameter reels because you can retrieve the line faster. But if you need to retrieve line quickly can't you strip it in faster than you can reel it in with any reel?

Gilman: Absolutely. A big fish will, generally, charge right at you sometime during the fight. And if a fish charges you, then you have to resort to stripping.

Q: What about expensive drag systems on reels, like disc drags?

Gilman: I don't like disc drags. The more line you have out the more resistance a disc drag will give you because the diameter of the line on the reel is smaller. When you use a disc-drag reel you need to stop and readjust your drag or you might lose your fish, especially if he's a big one. With a big diameter reel like a Loop the resistance is the same all the time so you don't have that problem.

Q: Putting big diameter reels aside for the moment, what do you think about click-drag reels?

Gilman: I think that for just standard fishing a click drag is better than a disc drag for most people. They'll get in less trouble with it. Once they get into a lot of big fish they ought to just skip the disc drag and go directly to a Loop reel. And if you need 'em you know where you can get 'em.

Rod Length

Q: Any other tips for folks buying tackle?

Gilman: As for rods in the West, longer is better than shorter. I like a stiff action, like the RPL type action, or the IMX. You know, there's just no point in having a real soft rod out in this country.

Q: Is that for the casting, for the fish catching or both?

Gilman: It's for the casting. As for the fish catching, with a soft rod you'll break fewer fish off, for sure.

But you can adjust for that. For instance, I fish threes and fours. My big rod is a four, a ten-foot, four-weight Sage. Now most people fish sixes and sevens, but the reason I fish a lighter rod is that I like a rod that's fine enough so that if I put all the pressure I can on that rod, even with a 4X or 5X tippet, it still won't break the fish off. That way I can really put the pressure to the fish, right down to the reel seat, without worrying about snapping the tippet.

Q: And do you fish a four-weight line on your ten-foot, four-weight rod?
Gilman: I fish one size over on all my rods. A five-weight line on a four-weight and a four-weight line on a three-weight. Weight-forward. Lining the rod that way makes it load easier.

Q: Not too many people use ten-foot rods.
Gilman: I love 'em. The older I get the longer I like a rod to be. The only problem is I've had to hire a little guy to go around with me and hold my ankles; because when that rod loads up I start going out in the lake with the rod. So somebody has to grab my ankles.

Q: Do you think that the length of a rod makes any difference in accuracy of casting?
Gilman: It depends on the distance. Say at 40 to 50 feet a nine-footer would be a little more accurate than a ten-footer.

So personally, if I had to win an accuracy contest, I'd go down and fish a nine-foot rod for that. And on the Beaverhead I like a nine-foot in the boat just because of the narrowness of the river. But man, I really like that ten-footer on the lakes and other big water.

Strike Indicators

Q: How do you feel about strike indicators?
Gilman: I'm all for 'em. I'm all for knowing what's going on down there, and if you can do it by watching the end of your line then that's fine. But I'm not a purist and I believe in strike indicators and I recommend that people use them.

Q: What kind of indicator do you like?
Gilman: I use the white Pulsa pinch-ons. I like the pinch-ons better than yarn because I think the yarn itself creates drag and affects the drift. I like the white ones because you can rough them up a little bit and they look like foam on the water.

114

Q: Do you think that's important, as opposed to fluorescent?

Gilman: Absolutely, because if you fish a place like over here on the Taylor River when the trout see those orange balls coming down the current they're gone. They're trained to them.

In addition to the white color, I like to use two indicators rather than one. I put them about a foot apart. The reason I use two of them is because sometimes you'll get a sideways strike and you won't notice it with one indicator, but you will with two. Also, with two indicators it's easier to find your indicator.

Nymphing Setups

Q: What kind of setup do you use under the water when you're nymphing?

Gilman: Back to the level leader, of course, and (depending on where I'm fishing and what I'm fishing for) generally I'll use a microshot around 18 inches from the fly. But over on the Taylor River you can't do that; your weight has to be at least six feet away from your fly or the fish won't take it. Because they're lead shy over there.

Q: What about using a weighted nymph under those conditions?

Gilman: The other thing I do is what we do in New Zealand. I tie a Pheasant Tail Nymph in a size eight, ten or twelve that is just total weight. It's heavily, heavily weighted and is really just a camouflaged sinker.

I tie one of those on and I tie onto the bend of its hook the fly that I expect to catch the fish on. That way, the fly I'm really hoping to catch the fish on isn't so heavily weighted and has more action. Also, it isn't as apt to get hung-up on the rocks as a weighted fly.

The weighted fly is all wrapped with pheasant tail so the fish either just let it go by or eat the fly behind it. And sometimes a fish does take the weighted fly.

Q: And how much tippet between the weighted fly and the other fly?

Gilman: A minimum of 18 inches. Depending on the fish, anywhere up to six feet, but generally about 18 inches.

Q: Do you have a rule of thumb as to the distance between the strike indicator and the lead weight?

Gilman: No, because there are things that make a difference, like the speed of the water. You have to figure it out when you get there. You either start short and work longer, or start long and work shorter, but you have to determine that new every day that you fish because of the different conditions.

No Hard and Fast Rules

Q: So the rule you often hear, 'twice the depth of the water', is incomplete because there are other factors?

Gilman: Exactly. The only real rule of thumb is that the terminal tackle is half the battle and you've got to fiddle with it long enough to get it right. That is, find out what's working at that place at that time. We may go around the bend and have to go through the whole process all over again. But that's the trick, not having a set of hard and fast rules. Those rules are what really screw people up. The whole trick is getting the fly to act natural.

Q: Does your own personal fishing technique differ from techniques that are generally accepted here in the West?

Gilman: That's hard to say because there are a lot of good fishermen out here and most of us are doing the same thing, and that's paying attention.

I would say that using the Pheasant Tail Nymph for a weight with a fly behind is something I don't see other people doing. Most people just use sinkers.

The dying of the lines is different. I don't see many people bother with dying their lines.

I think using a light, level leader below the indicator is real important. Very few people do that. Almost everybody tries to nymph with the same tapered leader they use for dry-fly fishing, and they're cutting their catch-rate in half.

And then a lot of the other things are the same, just like everybody else. Good equipment, good presentation.

Q: Do you have different techniques for different locales, like New Zealand versus the American West?

Gilman: As far as anything that adds to my ability to catch fish, I do it wherever I go. Like dying my fly line a dark color and taking the finish off my fly rods with steel wool. Those are things they commonly do in New Zealand. I'm conscious of anything that catches light. Your fly rod and line can catch the light and the fish will see it. And the dark-colored line makes a difference when it's on the water, too. I think maybe the fish are more apt to take the line for a stick or something natural floating by if the line's dark. You might even be able to line a trout with a dark line and get away with it.

Landing Fish

Q: What techniques do you teach in order to bring a fish in quickly?

Gilman: To bring a fish in quickly on a lake you want to let him run. You want to let him get tired as fast as you can, and you want him to make a couple of long runs.

On a river, if a fish heads up- or downstream, then instead of holding your rod up toward the sky you hold it horizontal and toward the closest stream bank. What this does is let the fish think he's winning. He's making his run but you're starting to put just a slight arc in what he's doing. You're slowly turning his head into shore. If he runs 30 feet up- or downstream, you might be able to move him 10 feet closer to your bank, and he doesn't even know it happened.

Also, always play large fish on a longer line. And when you're getting ready to beach any really big one, don't let your buddy run down there with a net or a camera. And don't try to land him with eight or ten feet of line; walk back up the bank, get away from your work a little bit. And when he wants to make that last good run, when you think he's through, be prepared to let him take it, to let him go.

Well, I think that's it. You've picked me clean. There's nothing else to learn from me.

Catch-and-Release

Q: Before I let you go I want to ask you how you feel about catch-and-release.
Gilman: Catch-and-release is a great principle but it needs to be applied to a certain cycle the stream is on. Catch-and-release is going overboard up on the Beaverhead and we're getting too many small fish now. They need to start getting some of those small fish out of there with a slot limit.

Q: What do you mean by small?
Gilman: Well, the 12- to 15-inch fish that are starting to take over. There's 3,000 per mile there right now.

Instead of having people keep the big fish, they should keep the little fish. You should put your breeders back and kill the young fish. Everybody's got that backwards; they all want to kill one nice big one and throw the little ones back, but that defeats their purpose.

God knows that we need catch-and-release, but it can't just be blindly applied to every stream.

Q: That takes care of my questions. Is there anything about the sport you want to add?
Gilman: Don't forget that we're all out there to have fun. That's the main thing. We're not out to break any records and fly fishing shouldn't be a competitive sport. So there really is no such thing as a bad fishing trip, is there?

I fish because it lifts my spirits and it does something for me that nothing else does. It turns my mind off and lets me just get back to nature for a while. If that's ever not there for me anymore, I'll quit fishing.

117

Al Troth

Where to reach him:

P.O. Box 1307

Dillon, Montana 59725

Phone: 406/ 683-2752

Professionally guides now: No. Retired from guiding in November 1996.

Homewaters: Beaverhead River, Big Hole River and Clark Canyon

Reservoir

Born: 1930, Pennsylvania

Where grew up: Pennsylvania

When started fly fishing: 1942

When came West: 1973, with vacation trips 1952-1973

Present fishing business affiliations: Al Troth Custom Tied Flies; "I do

some writing, sell a few photos and do some speaking

engagements."

When I arrived, on schedule, to interview Al Troth I located him in the large yellow-tan building behind his home on the edge of Dillon, Montana, across the street from Western Montana College. I knew I'd found Al's place when I saw a black-painted silhouette, about three feet tall, on the building's wall; the familiar, buggy profile needed no introduction, but was labeled Elk Hair Caddis. Al later explained that years ago his son, Eric—now a trout guide himself—had painted it for his dad.

After a, "Come on in," answered my knock on the door of the building, I found Al at his vise, revolving his bobbin around a partially completed leech pattern. He continued to tie, intermittently, throughout the interview, later moving on to tying up an order of Stimulators. Always the teacher, he pointed out to me that in tying the Stimulator he was using hackle two sizes under normal for the hook size, just as prescribed by Randall Kauffman, the fly's originator.

Al does his work in this building, and that work includes a substantial amount of photography. His photos appear regularly in a number of fly fishing and outdoor magazines. He does his tying in a generous-sized room with boxes of materials lining most of one wall. The boxes are labeled as holding hackles, various furs, gold wire and the like. A glance around the room and it was obvious that Al is a meticulously organized man. It appeared there was a place for everything.

After I settled in, putting my tape recorder on his tying table, the talk flowed. Al, a natural raconteur, needed little prodding from an interviewer; and thus our session was relaxed, seeming at times to be more a conversation than an interview.

We talked through a March morning. Our plan was for me to come back after lunch and take some photos of Al. When I returned with the cameras, Al had changed his shirt, putting on something he thought would photograph better. I took that as an indication of just what a thoughtful and considerate person he is.

Question: How did you get your start in fishing, Al?
Troth: When I was about 12 years old I was in a junior rifle club and the instructor, Toby Lakinmaki, was a fly fisherman. I learned to fly fish from him. He was a good fly fisherman, too, and a lot of the flies he bought were imported from England.

Q: So I guess you didn't go through the pole and worm stage like most of us?
Troth: No. I could see right away that fly fishing looked like a fun game. I can remember my first trout on a fly was a 14-inch brown trout on a Fan Wing Royal Coachman. Dry fly. That was on a little stream called Dunbar, in Fayette County, Pennsylvania.

119

Back then if I caught one or two trout that was fine. You know how fly fishing is. You pay the price: the more you fish, then the more you learn and the better you get. And if you're fortunate enough to have someone to help you out along the way, bully for you.

Q: When did you start guiding?
Troth: I started guiding in 1963. I taught school for 15 years in Pennsylvania, and I think I did a good job at it. But I burned out on teaching and just had to change. I moved to Montana and now I guess I'm a teacher on the Beaverhead.

Q: Do you enjoy teaching people to catch fish?
Troth: When I'm guiding I feel like I've caught all the fish myself. A client is landing a trout and I say to myself, "I'm catching that fish."

And I enjoy seeing the elation of people catching a big fish, of seeing them do everything right and land it. The look on their face is just amazing. The photos of people that I take with their fish usually show that; you can see them bubbling over. In fact one of my good customers called the other day and was kidding me about a print I had sent him of him and his wife. She's holding up a five-pound trout. He said, "I think it's better than our wedding picture."

Good Clients Like to Fish
Q: What kind of attitude do you like to see in your clients?
Troth: First of all, I like to fish with people who like to fish as much as I do. The reason I guide is because I enjoy being out and I just love seeing trout and I like to see them work even if I don't catch any. I go up on the river by myself a lot of days and just sit and watch fish rise and that part I enjoy. If people enjoy this sort of thing, or if they're not aware of it and I can tune them in to it, this is great.

Some people are always in a big hurry, though, and they come fishing with that same attitude. They want to catch a bundle of fish, and think that by hiring a guide they can almost guarantee that.

As a fisherman, you shouldn't put your expectations up too high. Some people expect miracles, but not everyone. A lot of people come in and tell me something like, "Hey, I live in Texas and get to fish one or two weeks out of the year; that's the only time I have a fly rod in my hand. I don't expect a lot. If I can catch a fish or two or even just work for some, that's dandy." And as a guide I feel that in itself is quite a good attitude. Then if I can put you into a dozen or two dozen fish that are in a 20- to 24-inch class that are visibly feeding, I've done the biggest part of my job.

Casting Deficiencies of Clients

Q: What deficiencies in fishing technique do clients commonly have?

Troth: Right from the start, number one, is casting. I don't care how accurate you are, I still think you should be able to cast at least 25 feet. We can catch every fish on our river here, the Beaverhead, if you can cast 25 feet. There's a limit as to how close you can get to a fish. All wild critters have a circle of fear and they only allow you to come in so close before you become a threat to them. So you have to be able to cast beyond that distance. It's amazing how many people can't even cast 15 or 20 feet.

Q: You only need to cast 25 feet?

Troth: You might have to cast farther if you're on a bigger river or if you're throwing streamers. For instance, casting Woolly Buggers on the Big Hole or the Bighorn you might have to cast more in the 40-foot range.

Beginners as Clients

Q: How do you feel about working with beginners?

Troth: That depends on how adept that person is at learning. A couple of years ago I had a father and son out who'd never cast before and had no idea how a fly rod worked. They'd never even seen anyone cast before, and of course they hadn't read anything. They showed up with really cheap equipment with the sales tags still on it. The rods, for instance, were the kind that were 9 feet long and had four guides on them.

They booked me for three days, and the first day the fish were really rising. Big trout. I think they caught two fish. At the end of the day I told them I couldn't charge them for the day's fishing. It wasn't in me. I told them to practice, to take some casting classes and learn how to cast reasonably well.

A day like that can be frustrating, but sometimes it's different if you can teach someone before the day is over to cast well enough to catch a few fish. And, really, I enjoy doing that.

For instance, I had one fellow come in with his wife. Neither of them fished, not even spincasting. They both wanted to go down the Beaverhead and catch some fish. His name was George.

I said to him, "I'll tell you what, George. I'll take about 10 minutes here on the driveway, and if I can teach you how to cast 20 feet I'll take you fishing. If not, we'll just forget about it." I use a cement block to teach casting, and I got him up on that.

Q: Why do you use a cement block?

Troth: Because if people try to use their body when they cast they keep falling off the block. They have to use the wrist.

So I had him up on the block. He picked it up right away. "You must play tennis or golf or something," I said. "Tennis," he said. We gathered up some stuff and went out on the river. The fish were working really well, and he managed to land something like 15 or 16 fish, which is not a bad day. The best fish he had was like 21 1/2 inches on a #16 Elk Hair Caddis. He fell in love with the sport. He gets better every year, and the last time he came he fished with a friend who was supposed to be a good fisherman, but George went like a bandit. He caught fish all over the place.

There were rules I had made for him on our first trip together: Locate a good place, get in position, make the cast far enough upstream of the fish so your nymph will get down as deep as the fish and will float by the fish naturally. Try to make the fly drift as though it weren't attached to your leader. That's the whole thing—dry fly or wet fly; the most successful technique is to make the fly behave like it's not hooked onto the end of your leader.

Well, he caught fish all day, and his poor friend, who was supposedly the expert of the two, caught two fish. And George just literally knocked them on their butt. He's really a good fisherman now.

Expensive Tackle Isn't Necessary

Q: I'm sure that clients show up with a wide variety of tackle and equipment. How important is it for a fisherman to have expensive stuff?
Troth: Having a good rod is real important. But every company has a couple of good rods, even the less expensive lines of rods. There are some $150 or $200 rods that are good if you know what you're looking for.

Q: What about reels with expensive drag systems?
Troth: Drag is the least thing. You want a smooth-running reel, that's about it. I can't say that I've used a drag for trout fishing. If you're playing trout on small, light tackle that drag can cause a lot of problems. When the fish gets farther away, then the drag should be changed, so you're better off not even playing with a drag. I think you're better off feathering the reel spool with your finger or a very light touch with your fingers on the line, always keeping your rod tip high. I don't think you need all the fancy drags they're building into these outfits. But the reel should be smooth-running so that the line comes off easily. There are plenty of good, inexpensive reels out there.

Q: Do people usually show up with good fly selections?
Troth: Often people show up with flies that are too big. Now we're catching pretty darned big fish on very small flies. And I feel that you may not land as many, but if you hook a fish and have him on for a reasonable length of time, even if the hook pulls out or something, you've had your place in the sun.

Smaller and Smaller Flies

Q: Why is it that we keep needing smaller and smaller flies to catch fish?

Troth: Here on the Beaverhead, excluding craneflies and terrestrials, most of our naturals are in the size 14 to size 24 range. So if you want to imitate what the fish are eating, then you'd best be fishing the same size. The Big Hole, on the other hand, has a lot of stonefly nymphs. The bottom of the Beaverhead is rubble and the Big Hole has a freestone bottom. The Big Hole has flat rocks and boulders galore, ideal stonefly water. If you pick up the boulders in the Big Hole you find stoneflies under almost every rock. And stoneflies are quite large.

So if you're fishing the Big Hole you'd better have some bigger flies with you. Stonefly nymphs in sixes and eights. If you're fishing the salmonfly hatch there, as big as #1 and 1/0s, long shank.

You can fish big attractor flies and big streamers, like Woolly Buggers, on the Beaverhead. We don't have a lot of sculpins in there but we do have ling minnows, which are pretty darned good fare for the trout because they're a non-spiny fish that must go down pretty smooth. And a lot of them are four or five inches long and as big around as your little finger. I've had clients catch fish and have them disgorge three or four ling minnows on the bottom of the boat.

So big Woolly Buggers and other streamers might do a job on trout feeding on other fish, but as far as insect-type flies go we don't use anything bigger than 14s.

Bringing Fish In

Q: What common mistakes in fishing technique does the average fisherman make?

Troth:—For one thing, people take too long in landing fish. So many times they get out there and they like to hear the reel go rrrr-rrrrr. In fact, I watch some of these TV fishing shows and I see people hook a good fish and just stay in one place, never move their position.

Q: What do you teach people about bringing a fish in quickly?

Troth: When I hook a big fish the first thing I do is get out on the bank and try to get below the fish so that the fish is fighting both the current and me, and the fish doesn't have all the advantage by hanging in the current. When I'm guiding I always try to get people down below the fish, downstream, whether they're on foot or in a boat.

In fact one day I had a well-known fisherman fishing with me and we had a big brown trout on. It measured 25 1/2 inches. We went probably half a mile downriver with that until I got it in a big backeddy, with dead water. And that's where we landed the fish. But up until then we had no choice of what to do. It ran under brush piles. I'd slide my finger down the leader and pretty soon I'd touch the fish and out it would go and here we go again.

All cases aren't like that, and usually it doesn't take that long. But it stands to reason that if you're playing a fish from upstream and he's hanging in the current, then you'd have as much difficulty in landing an old boot as you would that trout. So you either get across from him or downstream. And look for a quieter piece of water to get the fish into.

Q: At what angle should the fisherman hold the rod when landing fish?
Troth: That's a big problem. So many people get anxious and they drop their rod tip down and I know they're going to pop the leader. I always tell them to point the rod at the sky. I had one gentleman who was hell for breaking off fish. I taught him an object lesson by tying a fly onto a 6X leader and hooking it onto a fence post. I had him hold the rod tip up and see if he could break the leader, and he couldn't. Actually, I've done that with a lot of people, and they never can break it unless they lower their rod.

Presentation More Important Than Pattern

Q: What suggestions do you have for helping good fishermen get even better?
Troth: I think too many people, even good fishermen, exaggerate the importance of selecting the exact fly pattern. After having decent casting ability, being able to read the currents so you can make a drag-free presentation is the most important part of fly fishing. And people so often think they're getting a good, drag-free drift when they're not.

Not too long ago I was fishing with a client, a well-known outdoor writer. I put him on a good trout and he's casting away. "You're draggin'," I told him. He didn't see the drag. I said "Why don't you cast closer to the fish?" "No," he said, "I think it's the pattern."

About 45 minutes went by and the fish was still there. It was a nice brown, about 22 inches. He said that he'd tried every pattern he had, and I told him I still didn't think it was the fly. "You're casting too far above the fish and the fly is dragging by the time it gets to the trout," I said. He insisted I take the rod. "Here, let me see you catch it."

I took the rod. My philosophy is to make the first cast out where the fish won't see it but in the same run, and watch, just to see where drag sets in. That will give you an idea of how far above the fish you can cast and still have it free-floating by the time it gets to the fish. I threw it out there and there was drag almost immediately.

I said "Watch this. I'm going to throw a foot above the fish, but off to the left-hand side again, and watch how nice the fly will come by him then." I shortened up on the line and the fly came down beautifully, off to the side of the fish. "Now let's throw it over the fish," I said. I made a couple of false casts and the

124

fish came up and took a natural and I dropped the fly in the disturbance made by the fish. About a foot above him. He took it, and there it was. One cast.

I had the same kind of experience with another good fisherman. I fish with him every year. Like most people, he used to try pattern after pattern. Not any more. These days he doesn't say, "I think it's the fly pattern." When he's having trouble working on a fish he'll say, "God, I didn't get a good drift," or, "I'm having a hard time getting a natural drift on that spot."

I had to really prove all this the hard way to one client. We'd been trying to catch this big, female brown trout. The client had been casting to her for five hours, and the fish had been nymphing the whole time. I kept telling the client that the problem was presentation, he wasn't getting a drag-free drift. The client insisted that the problem was with the fly patterns. Finally, I said, "I'll tell you what. I'll make you a fifty dollar bet that I can take a bare hook, a piece of yarn from my sock, fashion a fly and catch that fish in ten casts or less. Fifty dollars." He says, "You're on."

So I took a knife and cut all the dressing off a fly so I had a bare hook, a regular shank #14. I was wearing a pair of those Army O.D. socks and I just pulled a piece of that O.D. yarn out and fashioned a fly, made a tail out of some of the yarn, did a double wrap for the thorax. I tied on the fly and cast it. I'd had plenty of time to study the currents, of course. On the fourth cast I had the fish. And the fifty dollars.

Q: Did he pay off?
Troth: He not only gave me the fifty dollars, he treated me to dinner that night, too. And our relationship got better from there on because there was another person who learned that presentation is probably the biggest part of this game.

Al McClane, the fishing writer, in an article called "Presentation, the Final Art," attributed 90 percent of fly-fishing skills to presentation for catching a fish with success. And I agree wholeheartedly with that.

Dries Easier Than Nymphs

Q: Regarding good presentation, do your clients find easier to fish with dry flies or nymphs?
Troth: There are more good dry-fly fishermen than there are good nymph fishermen. That's because with dries it's easier, you can see everything happening.

Q: But in nymphing you can see your indicator. Doesn't that help?
Troth: Yeah, but a lot of folks don't seem to realize that when that indicator is dragging so is the fly.

Special Casts

Q: Do you suggest that fishermen have any special casts in their repertoire?
Troth: I think the reach cast is probably one of the better casts to know. Also, what I call a lazy-S cast where you stop your rod abruptly and throw snakes into the line and leader. Really, with both of those casts what you're doing is mending in the air. I've never found the need for a whole lot more casts than that.

Q: Do you teach people to use a different casting technique when they're nymph fishing?
Troth: Yes I do, especially if you're fishing nymphs in a deep run, throwing weights and an air-resistant indicator.

If you do a lot of false casting with a rig like that you'll end up with tangles and spend the day re-tying it. But if, after your float, you let your fly continue to drift downstream, let it tighten up with the current at the end of the drift, and then you lift your rod tip a bit, you'll find that a simple flip of the rod tip will make a cast. If you're not requiring any long casts, this works out super because you just make an upstream flip without a backcast, and you're back in business. The fewer foulups you have on the terminal end of your tackle, the more pleasant your day's going to be.

Rod Preferences

Q: What is your personal rod and line preference as to both dry flies and nymphs?
Troth: I use a nine for a five, or a nine for a four with a five-weight line on it. With most graphite rods you can use a line size or two over what the maker recommends. I use the heavier line because I think that for shorter casts it brings out the action.

The weight system for lines is the weight in the first 30 feet of line, and if you're only casting 20 feet of line then your rod isn't going to work like it should. If you're casting 20 feet, and if your rod is designated for a #4 line, then the rod will work more like it should if you're using a heavier line, like a #5. So your average casting distance dictates what line weight you use, and I usually try to get as close as I can to a fish; that way I have more control over the cast both accuracy-wise and drift-wise.

Strike Indicators

Q: Do you use a strike indicator? If so, what kind do you prefer?
Troth: I use strike indicators and I prefer wool. I've fished both the natural wool and the synthetic versions, and I feel that the one works as well as the other. I dress mine well with fly dope. I don't put as much wool on as some people. Occasionally I see a great gob of it hanging down two or three inches from the knot. Mine are normally trimmed down to half an inch.

Q: How do you attach a yarn indicator? Do you use a loop in the leader and stick the yarn through it?

Troth: Yes, I put a knot in the leader and tie the yarn in. What kind of knot depends on what part of the leader you're tying it on. If you're tying it up real high then I use the knot that Lefty Kreh recommends with his yarn indicator. That works well with stiff, butt section material. But from the middle of the leader down to the terminal end I use a lark's foot.

With Lefty's knot I can reposition the yarn just by loosening the knot and sliding it, but with the lark's foot I take the knot out altogether and retie it.

Black Indicators

Q: How about color in an indicator?

Troth: I think that the colors of indicators are very important, and a lot of people aren't aware of the importance of black indicators. If you're using one of the wool indicators in any light color, including fluorescent orange, then it's translucent and the light goes through it. When light goes through the material the contrast is lessened. If you have black wool the light doesn't go through it and it forms a silhouette.

Last year I fished with a gentleman, good fisherman, and we were working over a big rainbow. It was raining, and he said, "Damn, Al, I can't see my indicator." He had a light-colored indicator. I tied on one of the black wool ones. I told him, "Try that." He made a cast off to the side of the fish and said, "Oh, great." He made two or three casts, I think, and he had the fish.

Using black for visibility is really a good idea on certain days and certain kinds of water. Like late in the day when the water's real silvery, that shiny, glassy water. That's when black is just outstanding. And the same thing's true for dry flies, as well.

Last year we had a couple of runs on the Beaverhead that in the evening would load up with trout taking spinners. It was shallow water, from four inches to a foot deep, and there would be maybe two dozen fish laying in there. They came in from a real deep run late in the evening, and the light was terrible after the sun had dropped over the hill. I had everybody fishing black-wing flies and I made a lot of converts.

Eleven-Foot Dry-Fly Leaders and Four-Foot Tippets

Q: What leaders and tippets do you like to use?

Troth: For dry flies, I use about four feet of tippet casting upstream to big fish. A long time ago the tippet was 15 inches to 20 inches long, normally. Since it's harder to straighten out four feet of tippet than, say, a 15- or 20-inch tippet, you're building in a slack line cast by using four feet of tippet. And that's on a

127

total leader length of about 11 feet for dry flies. I find myself using 11-foot leaders as a standard, almost.

For nymphing, I try to keep most of my leaders about the same length as the rod so that when I'm landing a fish I usually have the nail knot out of the rod tip.

Sometimes, for dry flies, even 11 feet is too short. Last year I got into some fish that were feeding on a midge hatch in the morning along with a PMD spinner fall, and I found myself using a 14-foot leader for dries because the water was clear and the fish were spooky. I had an outstanding day. I fished for nine fish; I caught and landed seven. They ran from 22 to 26 1/2 inches. They were caught on size 16 PMD spinners and size 18 midge patterns.

It was kind of funny. I went out two days later to the same spot and I thought I'd repeat that. I couldn't catch a fish. Could not catch a fish! I did everything the same, same flies. I don't know what it was, but things didn't work out quite right. That's one of the things that keeps us coming back, I think.

Only a Few Patterns Needed

Q: Given your emphasis on the importance of presentation, is it a corollary that a person doesn't need to carry lot of patterns to catch fish?

Troth: Yes, it sure is. If I had four of my own fly boxes lying on the counter and you looked into the boxes you would find that one box had maybe 150 Olive Pheasant Tails. You'd see a bunch of Flashback Hare's Ears. Some of these are in different sizes, but you only need about four patterns if you really want to go skimpy.

In addition to the nymphs, my Elk Hair Caddis would have to be on the list, along with a Parachute Adams. If I wanted to add something to that I'd add a Woolly Bugger or the leech pattern that I'm tying here *[Interviewer's note: the leech pattern in his vise has a brown Mohair body, brown marabou tail, brown hackle collar and brass bead head].* I fish the leech more than a Woolly Bugger because I do better with it.

The sizes of the patterns would vary with the season. As the season progresses the insects generally became smaller and smaller. So you should be carrying a bigger selection of small flies later in the season. Another reason for that is that the fish have been fished over more, are a little spookier, and small flies are a little easier to fool them with.

Designing Trout Flies

Q: Al, in the world of fly fishing, you've done it all—guide, fly-tier, fly-designer, expert fisherman, author and photographer; what do you consider your greatest contribution to the sport?

Troth: I'd have to say designing trout flies. I have a lot of patterns that people don't even know about. *[Interviewer's note: on Al's wall hangs a shadow-box* *of some of the flies that Al has designed. They are: Elk Hair Caddis, Olive Dun, Olive Scud, Al's Hair Hopper, MacSalmon, MacHopper, Gulper Special, Little Yellow Stone, Olive Pheasant Tail, Pale Morning Dun Flashback, Partridge and Peacock with Red Tag, Al's Hair Cricket, Hair Spider].*

Q: How do you approach designing a trout fly?
Troth: My philosophy on fly design is that certain flies, if viewed from underwater, have certain features that are important. Like with a stonefly you have a long, big body. That's the most important feature of that insect. You can take a live stonefly, pull the wings off and throw it in the water and the trout will eat it. The second most important part of that stonefly would be the legs, the third most important feature would be the wings. The antennae and the tails, they're not too important.

The Elk Hair Caddis

Q: Did you follow that philosophy in designing the Elk Hair Caddis?
Troth:—Yes, and the Elk Hair Caddis works so well because it imitates a lot of things. It can imitate a caddisfly, which it was designed for; it could imitate a small stonefly; and it could imitate an emerging mayfly. Tied in big sizes it could imitate a bigger stonefly or a big hopper. And we've caught a number of fish underwater with the Elk Hair Caddis after it finally did sink.

Q: Do details on a fly, like legs on a hopper, really make any difference?
Troth: Hard to answer. Sometimes they sure do. I remember in 1986 we had a fantastic hopper season on the Bighorn River. In 1983 I'd originated a fly called the MacHopper which had rubber legs. But the first occasion I had to really use it was in '86 during that great hopper fishing on the Bighorn. I was fishing with my son, Eric. We're coming down one of the first runs just below the put-in place at the dam, and he dropped the fly out. I can still see the thing happening. A nice big brown came up and hung under the fly. I said, "shake the rod tip." He shook the rod tip and the legs twitched a little bit, then POW, gone.

We had great luck twitching those rubber legs on that trip. But the trout in that river had been fished over so hard that they were looking for something to authenticate the naturalness of the hopper pattern. We had fantastic luck with that pattern the rest of the season.

Bright Colors On Flies

Q: Does it detract from a fly to add a bright color, like a fluorescent post on a Parachute fly?
Troth: Not really. It's rare now that I tie up an order of Parachutes that I don't do some fluorescent pinks along with the white posts and black posts. And if

129

they don't buy any white, they buy the pink. People need all the help they can get in seeing where the fly is. And I haven't found that the bright colors detract at all from the fishing.

Q: Is that because the fish doesn't see it or because he doesn't care?
Troth: I'm not sure, but I do know that if the fish had to examine closely every morsel of food that came down the river they'd starve to death.

Q: Would it be okay to make an Elk Hair Caddis with a wing of fluorescent pink elk hair?
Troth: That's all right, that's great.

Q: How did some of your flies other than the Elk Hair Caddis come about?
Troth: The Pheasant Tail is an unusual one. Frank Sawyer came up with the original Pheasant Tail. He tied it with just copper wire and pheasant-tail fibers. I added legs, I added a wing-pack, I added peacock and changed the color of it. In essence it was a different fly. If you buy a Pheasant Tail now, it is tied by the directions that I set forth. What Orvis, Umpqua and the shops you go into have is, in essence, my fly.

Tying the Troth Elk Hair Caddis

Q: In addition to designing new patterns, have you come up with any different techniques for tying flies?
Troth: Yes I have. In addition to designing flies, I've brought to light some old tying techniques that have now been accepted by modern tiers. One of those techniques I gleaned out of G.E.M. Skues' method of tying a fly he called "Little Red Sedge." That was a first part of the Elk Hair Caddis. I tied a Little Red Sedge, but instead of tying the wing that Skues tied, I tied elk hair for the wing.

His technique of using the brass wire to rib the hackle, though, is something I kept as a part of the Elk Hair Caddis. With that technique— instead of tying the hackle in at the back and winding it to the front— you tie the hackle at the front, wind it to the rear, and to hold it in place I come up to the front with a gold wire.

Q: Some people have trouble using wire to tie in the hackle in the Elk Hair Caddis pattern? What's your way of doing that?
Troth: I tie the wire on first, toward the back of the hook. Before I tie in the wire I cover the hook shank with tying thread from the eye down to the point where the fly's going to end, right above the barb. Then I tie down a piece of wire there. Next, I tie the dubbing on, moving toward the eye. I tie in the hackle at the front and wind it back. I secure the hackle at the rear by a couple of

winds of wire, then bring the wire forward, winding in the direction opposite to the direction I wound on the hackle. Then I secure the wire at the front with the tying thread.

Randall Kauffman uses the same technique in his Stimulator fly. He gives me credit for the idea in his book. That same technique is being used not only with wire now, but with tinsels, with monofilament and a lot of things. When I tie Woolly Buggers, for instance, my Woolly Buggers will outlast anybody's because I tie the hackle in the front, wind it to the rear and come up through it with some clear mono.

Parachute Posts the Troth Way

Q: You have an interesting way of tying posts for Parachutes, too, don't you? Will you tell us about that?

Troth: Yes, my way is rather different. I lay a piece of Antron wool across the hook, like I was going to tie on a spinner wing. I secure that with a couple of figure-eight turns of thread. Then I spin the wool wing around so it's on the bottom of the hook. Next I pull both ends to an upright position and wind the tying thread around its base, 10 to 12 turns, and a couple of turns in front and back. This method of tying a post is the only way I tie parachute wings now. It allows me to tie Parachutes in very small sizes without excessive bulk in the body area.

Q: You're by no means a newcomer to fly tying, are you?

Troth: I've been doing this for a whole lot of years. And I had a good teacher, Toby Lakinmaki, that same Finlander who was my rifle coach when I was a boy in Pennsylvania. The flies he bought from England were extremely well-tied, and I took them apart to see how they were made. There weren't many books on the subject then. If you bought a kit, there was a set of instructions on how to tie a fly printed on the inside of the lid of the box. That was about it.

I tied for some pretty notable people in the East. John Alden Knight and his son, Richard. The son paid me what I considered a nice compliment in his book on trout fishing; he said that he thought that the three leading exponents in the field of nymph design and tying were Ernie Schwiebert, George Harvey and Al Troth. Which I considered a real compliment.

Synthetic Tying Materials

Q: How do you feel about using synthetics in fly-designs? Do you have any prejudice against using them?

Troth: No, no prejudice at all. Whatever works is OK. I tie stonefly patterns with a wing made out of FlySheet. I buy it from John Foust over in Hamilton, Montana. For instance, I use it on the Little Yellow Stonefly that I tie, and I use it on grasshoppers as well. On the LeTort Hopper, for instance, instead of using turkey I'll use the FlySheet material. You might ask, "Why don't you use brown turkey?" I say, "Because brown turkey costs $4.95 a pair." So that's why I don't use the turkey anymore.

And there are synthetics like my friend John Betts came up with, like Z-lon. And Micro Fibetts for tails; boy, they're labor saving.

Bead Head Flies

Q: Some people, purists, steer clear of bead-head flies. How do you feel about them?

Troth: Oh, I like them just fine. They've fallen right into the picture. The beads used to be hard to find, but now they're all over. I use nickel-silver or gold, and the gold would be brass, naturally. I also tie some black-bead Bugger type patterns for lake fishing.

And lead, compared to brass, is about 25 percent heavier so you could use lead as well as brass, and have a smaller profile, if you want it. Of course, lead is toxic and isn't allowed in Yellowstone Park. I weight all my flies now with brass or copper only.

Q: Why are bead-heads so effective?

Troth: Bead-heads are successful because they get down there. They swim in a nice way. Before beads, I used to put a little shot right in front of the clinch knot, and that worked just as well. Didn't look as good, but worked just as well. You know, if you're thinking a little bit you could have a little box full of beads in your vest and right out on the stream you could slip a bead over your tippet, tie on a fly without a bead head and you've got a bead-head. It'll work much the same way. The bead will slide right down next to the fly all the time.

One reason bead-heads are so popular is because more people are getting into nymph fishing. As a professional fly tier, I find myself tying fewer dry flies the last couple of years, and more nymph patterns, and that indicates to me that the angling public has discovered nymph fishing and how productive it can be.

Benefits of Catch-and-Release

Q: Turning our attention from catching trout to letting them go, do you approve of catch-and-release?

Troth: I think catch-and-release is here to stay, without a doubt, and I think it's a great thing. Being on the river every day and releasing fish every day, I see something a lot of people don't realize about trout. If the water conditions are stable the same big trout will occupy the same feeding lie every day. There are trout, big fish, that we've caught again and again. One in particular comes to my mind that we caught eight times in the month of August last year. The fact that we caught him seven times after the first time he was released is sort of a tribute to our handling of the fish and the sport that can be gained by releasing fish. So enough said right there.

I mean we turn fish loose every day that we've probably caught before and released before. A lot of people in the coffee shop kid me. They say, "Al, you've got all your pets named and numbered out there."

Q: Do you find yourself doing that?
Troth: Yeah, you do really.

Q: Do you have trouble getting clients to release fish?
Troth: I haven't had anyone kill a fish in the last ten years. If someone wants to have one mounted I tell him that I'll take a super good picture of him with the fish and then he can lie about the size of it.

Q: Do you ever keep trout, kill them to eat them?
Troth: Yes I do. On Clark Canyon Lake. It's a little different story there. Those are stocked trout, and the state is going to stock a quarter million fish every year there, so you might as well take your share and eat 'em. I have no qualms about that.

How to Fool a Fish With a Fly, In a Nutshell

Q: Do you have any final Words of Wisdom for our readers?
Troth: If I were, in a very few words, to tell somebody how to fish a fly I would say, "Make the fly behave as though it weren't attached to your leader. Period."

How do you do it? I don't care. If you have to use a special kind of cast, mend, or stand on your head, that's fine. But if you can get that thing to dead drift without any movement from the leader then you'll catch fish. Now there are times when a worked fly will maybe do a little bit better, but I find that to be unusual compared to good, consistent dead-drifting principles.

If you can make a dry fly go downstream without dragging, and can tell that it's not dragging, and if there's a fish working and you get by him enough times, then you'll most likely catch him.

One of the other things I find is that somebody will put a fly on and make five casts and say "Didn't take it. Something's wrong with the fly." I'll say, "Well, what's wrong with all the naturals going by the fish that he's not eating?" And you can see the look on their face.

If the fish was eating every insect that came by and if one passed him by he'd chase it down just so he didn't let even one get away, and then you threw your fly out there and he didn't take it, then I'd say, "Okay, something's wrong." But when there's three or four naturals on each side of his nose and he's eating one here and one there, then there's nothing wrong with your fly. You just haven't given it enough opportunity to be successful.

Paul Roos

How to locate him:

Paul Roos Outfitters

326 N. Jackson

P.O. Box 621

Helena, Montana 59624

Phone: 406/442-5489 or

800/858-3497

Fax: 406/449-2293

Professionally guides now: Yes

Homewaters: Smith River, Blackfoot River, Missouri River and Rock

Creek

Born: Lincoln, Montana, 1942

Where grew up: Lincoln, Montana

When started fly fishing: About age 7

Other fishing business affiliations:

North Fork Crossing Lodge

P.O. Box 179

Ovando, Montana

Phone: 406/793-5046

Fax: 406/793-5058

This interview with Paul Roos took place in the dining room of his comfortable home in Helena, Montana. We met downtown at his Orvis fly shop, Cross Currents, then drove to his house because Paul said we'd have fewer interruptions there. I arrived at Cross Currents as the shop was opening, and we ended our session about two o'clock in the afternoon.

Paul is thorough and organized, and early in the interview it was apparent that he was prepared to answer my questions. He'd done his homework. It was equally apparent that he is blessed with the gift of teaching and is a leader of men; as we talked I sensed that my role as interviewer was subtly shifting to include the roles of pupil and potential enlistee in the conservation wars, as well.

Before our interview I'd known that Paul was a conservationist as well as a highly respected fly-fishing professional in the Helena area. I wasn't prepared, though, for the depth of dedication he projected. If the world were to be divided into givers and takers, Paul would surely be among the givers. For him, it is not enough commitment of his time to earn a living in the fishing business as guide and entrepreneur; he also chooses to spend significant time and energy as an environmental activist, protecting the rivers and streams of his home state. And not just on an organizational level. He customarily and regularly dukes it out with industries and organizations whose interests would damage the fisheries of Montana. As fishermen, we can all be grateful to him and to men like him.

Question: *How did you get started guiding, Paul?*
Roos: I began guiding with Pat Barnes in West Yellowstone, Montana, in 1967. I guided with him for three years, then my wife and I went back to Lincoln, Montana, my hometown, and started our own outfitting business. We've been outfitters since then.

I'm also a teacher, and was principal of the school in Lincoln for five years until I moved to Helena in '76. I taught in Helena until I retired in 1994, guiding and outfitting on the side. Gradually the tail began to wag the dog, and I had to make a choice between teaching and the fishing business. As a result, in 1994, we expanded Paul Roos Outfitting to a full-time operation and opened an Orvis fly shop, Cross Currents, in Helena. More recently we've built North Fork Crossing, a guided fishing lodge on the Blackfoot, and we sold Cross Currents in 1997.

Q: *What do you like about guiding?*
Roos: The attraction, originally, was that I saw guiding as something that would work well in the summertime when I wasn't teaching. Mostly I liked

earning a living doing what I enjoy, and that's being out on rivers and streams. What has kept me in it is the people. I enjoy the clients, the guides and even my competitors.

Q: Do you do much guiding these days?
Roos: Yes I do, but I don't think I'll ever guide more than 70 or 80 days a year. I feel that you've got to be careful not to lose touch with what makes you an "expert," that you've got do some fishing on your own. And you've got to stay in touch with different waters.

Tomahawk Creeks

Q: Other than the Missouri, what waters do you fish and guide on?
Roos: We fish the Blackfoot, the Little Blackfoot, the Smith, the Clark's Fork, the Upper Clark's Fork and Rock Creek. We have a lot of other water that we fish that we generally refer to as "Tomahawk Creeks." These are waters that we're not talking about in our publications because they're special spots and they need to be protected from people finding out about them. I do an awful lot of those.

Q: I don't guess you want to mark any of those on my map, do you?
Roos: No, but the Blackfoot was a Tomahawk Creek until The Movie came out. I think we were the first outfitter on the Blackfoot. If not the first, one of the first. We fish it from Ovando down to the Roundup Bar, and some times of the year almost down to Bonner.

Q: How much experience should a person have before taking a guided fishing trip?
Roos: I've got some real strong feelings about that. I believe that the only thing that you need in order to enjoy a day with me is willingness to enjoy the experience and to learn. I like to teach, so a beginner can be the most fun for me. I also enjoy guiding a very advanced fly fisher who recognizes, as I do, that the more you learn the more you have to learn. Then I have the opportunity to go to that upper level and deal with the technical aspects that you never touch on with 70, 80 or 90 percent of your clients.

How to Adjust For Success

Q: What's the difference between the fly fisher with medium skills and those of a more advanced fisherman?
Roos: The difference is that the more advanced fishermen can catch the tough fish. They know how to approach him, they know what didn't work. If they're not succeeding they've got a pretty good idea of what to do next. Most fly fishermen don't really understand what they need to do next if things aren't work-

136

ing. With them it's a guess, like change the fly. Or change the color of the fly, and that may be way down the line in terms of what they ought to be doing.

Q: What should a fisherman do when he or she isn't having success? What changes should they make in their tackle or technique?
Roos: Here's how I think you should approach the problem of not catching fish. I believe you should consider these things in this order:

1) Consider whether you might be getting drag. If you are, or might be, then you either lengthen your leader or your tippet or switch to a smaller diameter tippet, or both. This would apply to both dry-fly and nymph fishing, but not necessarily to streamer fishing.

2) Change size and profile of your pattern. You can change to a smaller or larger fly. Or if you're using a Humpy or Goofus Bug—which has a short, fat profile—you might want to switch to something with a long, narrow profile, like a stonefly or caddis pattern. I find that sometimes you might be in the right size range, but need a different profile.

3) If none of the above pay off, try changing the medium. In other words, if you're fishing on the surface, go to nymphing; if you're fishing a nymph, maybe you should go to an emerger. I consider there to be three mediums: right in the film, on the surface, and down below the surface at various depths.

4) If you know you're in the right medium then, finally, you might want to consider changing the color of your fly.

People Think About Fly Color First
Q: That's not the way most people usually try to solve the no-success problem, is it?
Roos: No. Generally, it's always color. The first thing people say is something like, "I'll try this green one." Not always, but almost always people will zero in on color. I don't think color is nearly that important.

Q: Is that because the other factors, like drag, are so much more important or because trout aren't usually that selective?
Roos: I think both of those things apply. There are times when color is important, but it's way down on the list.

Q: When are those times?
Roos: Either there's an ongoing hatch or there's a history of a hatch that's been going on for a number of days.

Nymphing
Q: You were discussing what changes in fishing technique people should

137

consider when they're not catching fish. Do you have any ideas like that which are special to nymph fishing?

Roos: Yes I do. When you're nymph fishing it's a brand new set of rules from dry flies. If you're nymph fishing and not catching fish then the first thing you change is the distance of your indicator from the fly, and if you're using the end of your line as the indicator then you lengthen or shorten your leader.

Here again, I think the usual mistake people make is casting too long a line. When you cast short you've got so much more ability to manage the line so as to get a dead drift rather than unnatural drag. That's very difficult to do with a real long line. The further out you get, cross current, the less able you are to deal with drag.

Long Casts Not Desirable

Q: Earlier you mentioned the differences between experts and average fishermen. Where do casting skills fit into that difference, especially the ability to cast a long line?

Roos: Some of my experts aren't what I'd classify as great casters, but they're great fishermen. Most of the time, in my opinion, the great casters go into the mediocre category as to ability to catch fish. And when I say great casters, I'm talking people who cast long distances when they fish. Many of these folks have the skill to cast short and to cast well, but they don't.

Q: Why don't they cast short or well?

Roos: Most of them think distance casting is what all good fly fishermen do, that if they *can* cast long they *should* cast long,

Others of them know that they shouldn't be casting so long but they do it anyway because they enjoy it. And that's okay, so long as they know that they're reducing their ability to catch fish by casting long all the time.

Q: Why does casting a long distance cost you fish?

Roos: There are two main reasons. First, the more line you use the more current you're casting over and therefore the more drag you're apt to get. Second, it's more difficult to hook the fish if you've got a lot of line out there.

Fishing Flat-Water Hatches

Q: How do your fishing techniques differ from those of other good fishermen?

Roos: One example is how I fish hatches on flat water, like the Missouri, which is a tailwater fishery. We often have profuse hatches of small insects there and the fish get in pods, two to four inches under the surface of the water. Just sipping. To catch them you need supreme accuracy because, being so close to the surface, they have a very small window.

138

My opinion varies a great deal from many experts on how to fish that kind of situation. I think the best way to do it is to get in close, 90 degrees from the fish, by wading on your knees or wading deep so you have a real low profile. Then you use a quick little wrist cast and a very straight line. If you get good at it you can almost get the fly over that fish every time.

Q: How far are you casting with your 90 degree method?
Roos: About twenty feet from my body to where the fly lands. That's very short. You can't use the 11- or 12-foot leader that I usually use, or even a nine-foot leader. You have to use a 7 1/2-foot, otherwise you're casting all leader. Sometimes I get even closer, but about 12 to 15 feet would be about as close as I'd want to get. I cast about two feet in front of the fish, and bring the cast down real low—you don't cast high that close to the fish. If you do you'll spook 'em with that movement up in their cone of vision. So you bring the fly in real low, but not as low as a side cast because you can't get good accuracy with a side cast. Then you drop the rod tip.

You only need about three inches of drag-free float because the window's so small. As soon as it goes by him you pick it up, then cast again, then again. Very effective. And you can teach beginners to do that pretty fast.

Better Than Down-and-Across

Q: What do the other experts say to do in that situation?
Roos: Most of the experts say you should fish down and across. That takes a longer line, is less accurate and much more time consuming than fishing close at 90 degrees.

With the down-and-across method you're upstream of the fish and the current will carry your disturbance of the water down to them, so you need to stay farther away. By staying far away, you're casting farther and not apt to get a cast in that small window.

Also, with down-and-across you have to take the time to let the line float away from the fish after the float, then retrieve it, and all that takes a lot of time. Using my position of 90 degrees from the fish, you can get about 10 floats over the fish in the time you'd get one float with the down-and-across method.

Q: Are long casts ever desirable?
Roos: Well, with streamers, yes. With streamer fishing it's often advisable to cast long because then you're covering more water with your retrieve. Plus, you're not so worried about drag.

As far as dry-fly fishing, there are times when it makes sense to cast long because of the fact that you can't, for some reason, get any closer. Especially if there is a fish there and you're a good enough caster to get it right over him.

Then go ahead and use your ability to cast long.

And if you're in still water the length of cast doesn't make a lot of difference because you don't have currents and drag to worry about.

Shotgun and Roll-Roll Casts

Q: Do you have any special types of casts that you like to use, any unusual casts?

Roos: Yes I do. One cast I've come up with is something I call a shotgun cast, and I may have gotten it from a client. I use it to fish a pocket behind a big rock, with currents going every which way, mostly when I'm fishing from a boat. I'll use a high-floating fly, and I'll put that real long leader to use by driving the line and leader into the water, piling the leader up into a mess, all 15 feet of it. Then I mend the line, mend the line, mend the line, and you can get a real long float in behind the rock, in the pocket downstream of it. It's a wonderful way to fish behind a rock. You're fishing maybe 25 feet of line and leader but you're casting it 12 feet. With that much leader curled out there that you can do a power mend on it and it doesn't affect the float of the fly.

Q: You don't use that cast when you're wade fishing?

Roos: No, but I use a similar technique wade fishing where there's a fast current and a large rock. I've come up with what I call the roll-roll cast, and I'm pretty damned sure I invented this one. You get 90 degrees to the rock and as close as you can get without spooking the fish, and that's usually not an issue because it's such a disturbed surface. You cast upstream of the rock with a lot of line and then pull the fly so it floats by the near side of the rock. Just as it's passing you roll cast the fly with a normal roll cast, and you put the fly in below the rock, but before the roll cast completes itself you roll cast again. That lays a great big belly of line upstream in the fast current.

Then you can just power mend—which is almost like a roll cast—and keep mending. And that fly just hangs in there below the rock. This fast current's taking your line and you flip it up, flip it up and it's a fantastic way to fish that kind of water. I can go in and fish that kind of water after a damned good fisherman and pick up all kinds of fish. The leader length has to be long for that, 15 feet, and I'd use about a 30-inch tippet.

Fishing Rules to Follow

Q: If you could have a few rules for people to follow to catch more fish, what would they be?

Roos: First, I would ask them to come to fly fishing with the idea that you want to enjoy the experience and to forget numbers and size. "Numbers and size" thinking detracts from what fishing is all about.

The second would be to stop and think what to change when the fish aren't coming to your fly. I talked about that earlier.

Q: What other rules for folks to follow?
Roos: The third rule is to come to a guided fishing trip ready to learn something, no matter where you're starting from. There are a few people who don't do that. They pay what I think is an exorbitant price to hire a professional guide and then they don't use the guide's knowledge. Those are the clients that I least enjoy, and I think that would be close to a unanimous opinion among guides.

Landing Fish

Q: What do you teach people about landing fish? Any rules you'd like to share with us?
Roos: So many people hold the rod too tight and when a big fish does something surprising to them they break it off right there. I use a technique fighting big fish, five pounds and up, that involves holding the rod with the pointer finger and thumb only, keeping the rod 90 degrees to the line. I teach people to use that technique during the part of the fight when the fish sort of hangs, and you're not sure what he's going to do next.

If you just have the rod with those two fingers and the fish takes off quickly, then the rod automatically bends toward the fish because you don't have the strength to hold the rod back. If it jumps toward the fish, that's the angle you want your rod to be.

Q: Anything else about landing fish?
Roos: With a good size fish it's very important to keep changing the plane of the rod on him, to move it from side to side continuously. That can really help you gain line on a fish. Bear in mind that when you're pulling parallel to the fish you're giving him an advantage; you want to be pulling 90 degrees to the current and to the fish whenever possible, and you change the plane of the rod to be able to do that. That gets the fish in much, much quicker.

Q: How about changing your position, moving to a different place, after you hook a fish?
Roos: If you're in a boat the number one thing is to row toward the fish and toward slow water. If you're wade fishing, then be willing to go downstream. Walk down the bank and try to get that 90 degree advantage to the current and the fish.

And with smaller fish, I get 'em in right away. There are people who enjoy listening to the reel sing, and that's okay, but you've got to recognize that every second you keep any fish on the end of your line you're putting stress on that fish. And personally, I don't get a big kick out of fighting fish. I get a kick out of getting them to take and setting the hook. I could probably do without setting the hook. I've actually thought about cutting the total bend of my hooks off. Raise and release, you might call it.

Mistakes In Tackle Selection

Q: How important is expensive tackle? What mistakes do you see people make in selecting tackle and equipment?

Roos: Let's start with reels. An expensive reel is probably the least important thing in trout fishing, in my opinion. About all a drag on a reel needs to do is keep the line from coming off too fast and developing an overrun. Reels can be sufficient for trout fishing if they just store line and run relatively smoothly and don't stutter. There's a myriad of good reels out there that cost about $40 or even less that are sufficient. When you go anymore than that with trout fishing then you're gaining very little.

Q: Where should you put that money you save?

Roos: I think in the rod. I think a high-quality rod really does improve a person's chances. I don't think you always need to go to a premium $400 to $500 rod. I'm not saying that. But when you go up from the $200 rod often—but not always—what you're getting is facade. Different guides, different wrappings, different finish, different reel seat and they're prettier. On the other hand, I think people make a mistake when the buy a $39 outfit at K-Mart.

Q: Do you think the average fisherman needs more than one rod for the various types of trout fishing around here?

Roos: I think that for this area two rods are sufficient. You can almost get by with one now, but you'd be pushing it a little bit. A 5-weight is closest to the best single rod now for this area. I prefer, though, to suggest that a person have two rods, either a 3 and a 5, or a 4 and a 6.

As for length of rods, when you're fishing other than small, small streams, I really think you should have an 8 1/2 or 9-foot, and I prefer the 9-foot length for better line control.

Q: What do you think about one- and two-weight rods?

Roos: I think they're great if somebody can afford to have special rods for special occasions. They add to the enjoyment of fishing, and a good fisherman can get a fish in almost as fast as on a larger rod. That's because the time of landing a fish depends more on tippet size than the weight rod you're using.

142

Preferred Dry-Fly Patterns

Q: In your own fishing do you carry a lot of patterns or just a few? And if you had to carry just a few dry-fly patterns, what would they be?

Roos: I believe that if you select in terms of size and profile you can really keep the number of flies you pack around with you down to a minimum. I try to do that.

If I were to cut my dry-fly selection down to the bare bones, there are some patterns I wouldn't go on the stream without, and here they are:

Parachute Adams. I really like the Parachute Adams, in sizes 18 through 14. I think that's a pattern everybody ought to have. It's popular because of visibility for the fisherman and, personally, I don't think the profile on a split-wing is as attractive to the fish as a parachute. Especially with mayflies. The Parachute Adams is a damned good mayfly pattern. And for visibility for the fisherman you can have the post in black or some bright color like fluorescent pink or lime. Another parachute pattern I like is a Parachute Hopper.

Stonefly/caddis pattern. You can use an Elk Hair Caddis for a stonefly hatch if the size is right, and vice versa. It's the shape more than anything. There is a fly called a Maki Stone, made by John Maki, a competitor of mine who lives right here in Helena. Real low profile, Muddler head, sparsely tied elk hair over the back, and a closed-cell foam body. It floats low in the water but doesn't sink. It's a killer fly. We usually use that one in size six and size four.

Caddis flies. The caddis I like best is the CDC caddis emerger, generally in a dark brown. It's a really great pattern. You can fish it in the film, you can pop it and fish it on the surface, you can skitter it a little bit. Generally I use that in 14s and 18s. It's surprisingly easy to see. I packed it in my box for a year and I didn't use it because I didn't think I'd be able to see it, but you can.

Goofus Bug. I wouldn't go anywhere without a Ginger Goofus. From 16s to 4s. You know what a Goofus is; it's like a Humpy but tied a little rougher. I started out with Pat and Sig Barnes and they tied the Goofus that way. It didn't look as pretty to the fisherman as, say, the Jack Dennis Humpy. The Jack Dennis Humpy had the nicely tied hair all doubled back, it looked like it came right out of Macy's.

I'd want the Goofus in brown hackle, light tan elk hair and then a variety of body colors, and my favorite is green if I had to go just with one. But it's nice to have a variety of body sizes, too. The Goofus Bug is extremely visible, and if it's tied well is a real hardy fly and will float like a dream.

I mention the big sizes, like four, because on freestone streams, on a slow day, if you want to fish dry for big fish that's the way to do it. You fish the big water—the big, fast, deep water—with a monstrous goddamned split-wing. And the Goofus is the one I'd use. They're hard to cast, and I generally use a 3X tippet.

I like to have those big flies tied so that the profile would be a size four, but the hook would be a six or an eight. Then it really floats high. It just sits up there, and the fish looks up and sees a bunch of refracted light on the surface and something that's damned big and they will move farther, and more aggressively, for something like that than they will for a Parachute Adams or even a Hopper.

Attractor Patterns. I guess I'd definitely want either an H & L or a Royal Wulff in attractor patterns. They're both real good. I'd go clear to size 20 on those and up at least to a six or a four, and I'd probably skip the 12. Also, the Stimulator is basically a stonefly, caddis, hopper attractor and is a good fly.

That takes care of the dry flies.

Soft Hackles

Q: How about soft hackles?

Roos: The only soft hackles I use are the CDC patterns. They're mostly just a body and some CDC feathers. There's no wing, and the CDC is like a long hackle laid down flat over the body, all the way around. Like you would a partridge feather on a conventional hackle. There's no tail. I know that the soft hackle is a great fly; I just don't fish 'em that much.

Nymph Patterns

Q: What nymphs do you like?

Roos: My favorite is the—you probably guessed it—Gold Ribbed Hare's Ear. I use sizes 18 to 10, both weighted and unweighted. I think it's a pretty darned good pattern for caddis larvae, fished down on the bottom; I use the big sizes, weighted, in freestone streams where there are stoneflies.

I'd want to have a Bead Head Caddis Pupa, in brown, sizes 16 and 14. And without a doubt, I'd include the Bitch Creek, in sizes six and eight. I fish those in freestone streams, dead-drift, even though people do strip them successfully. That's a fly I will not use an indicator on. It's such a big, heavy fly that it takes too much indicator.

Incidentally, an advantage to not using an indicator with any nymph is that you can fish different depths without changing your setup. You can simply let the tip of your line go down and you just watch whatever amount of line you've got out there on the surface. Nymph fishing that way is difficult, but it can be learned. You just have to do it a lot.

Q: Any other nymphs?

Roos: I guess I wouldn't be caught dead without a few Princes and some Pheasant Tails. In Pheasant Tails I generally use the real small ones, size 16 to 20, and I generally fish 'em tight line so that they're swinging just a little bit. Not a lot, just a little bit, moving cross-current just enough so that it's not

144

drifting naturally. I almost always fish that fly in the riffles on an emergence of mayflies. I'll fish it real shallow with a tight line and no weight. As for the Prince, I fish those anywhere from 10s to 14s. Usually weighted, dead-drift. That's a great whitefish fly, so if you're getting your butt kicked you can always get a little activity and hope the clients lose them before they know what they are. "God, that was a great rainbow!"

Whitefish on the Fly
Q: Do clients ever like catching whitefish?
Roos: Most beginners enjoy it, and even the advanced would rather catch a whitefish than nothing. So long as their friends don't see 'em do it. Hell, I'm the same way. I'd rather catch whitefish than nothin'. And some of those big ones will fight just like a brown. We've had clients on the river who just wanted to eat some fish and we've at times kept some whitefish, filleted them and cooked them just like trout. They're good.

And this brings up a point. I think that there's going to be a day—and I may be one of the first to say it—where fishing for carp and whitefish with flies becomes a sport that's not looked down on. The whirling disease may force us into those sorts of things. The carp is a great fighter and will take streamers, but with a dry fly they're extremely difficult to catch. It's accuracy and timing and very sporty. And they sure do fight.

Streamers
Q: How about streamers? Do you have any favorites?
Roos: The absolute, number one, unquestionable first choice is the White Marabou Muddler.

Q: White Marabou Muddler? I was sure you'd say Woolly Bugger, just like the rest of us. Why the White Muddler?
Roos: No, not the Bugger. The unweighted, White Marabou Muddler, in size two. I like long marabou behind the bend, about 3/4 longer than the length of the hook. It's a great fly. It's good for browns, but the rainbows generally prefer a black.

Q: How do you fish the White Marabou Muddler?
Roos: Fast. Strip it to beat hell. But if you're fishing in really cold water or warm water, then you've got to slow up. If it's real cold or warm you can let it go dead-drift. But in optimum water temperatures I move it like a freight train. I like to use a Hi-Density, full-sinking line so you can fish it shallow or fish it deep. It's a great shallow-water fly. You tell people to cast into shallow water, the inside of a bank, on a bright sunny day. Pebble bottom and clear, shallow water. They'll say, "Yeah, sure." They cast and BOOOM!

Double-Headed Hammer Casting

Q: Do your fishing and guiding techniques differ much from the techniques of other good fishermen and guides?

Roos: I think so. In addition to what I've already talked about—fishing flat water 90 degrees on the hatch, fishing short line, piling up my leader and doing a lot of mending in freestone streams—I vary from others in casting and in teaching casting technique.

In teaching casting I use the analogy of a double-headed hammer. I say to imagine you're standing in a door jamb and are trying to hammer a nail in front of you and a nail behind you. In both driving nails and casting you get your power from the forearm and then you finish with the wrist.

You stand in that door jamb—a narrow door for a short cast and a wider door for a longer cast—you tap the front nail then you come back and tap the other one. What that does is to teach them a technique of casting that works better for wind because it gives a real tight loop and a lot of power. I am without doubt a power caster, and almost all of my guides that I've taught are power casters. A lot of energy, a lot of line speed. Sometimes, of course, you don't want a tight loop and you want it to sort of die out there. But for basic casting motion I work on people leaving their body totally out of it and working on the forearm and getting elbow travel. The longer the line, the more elbow travel you've got. With a real, real short line it's almost all wrist, but you still have that forearm involved. You can cast a leader only with just wrist. It works fine.

Keep the Fly On the Water

Q: How about your guiding techniques, taking folks on the water? How do they differ from other guides?

Roos: As far as my guiding technique, my emphasis will almost always be on keeping the fly in the water. My basic premise is: don't pick your fly up to cast again unless you've got a damned good argument as to why you did. People cast too much. They've always got their fly in the air; they take their fly off the water too quickly and too often. Another foot or two of float might have picked up a fish but they pick up the fly while they still have a good drift going.

Another thing I teach is re-floating a fly instead of re-casting it. A lot of times you can re-float, and by that I mean a power mend that moves the fly, maybe as much as two feet, but you by God move that line so that when you drop it again you're into another float and that's a lot quicker than casting.

That technique is generally when fishing from a boat, but I use it wading, too. In big water, where I need to use a longer line, I'll power mend when I start to get drag. And moving the fly doesn't seem to bother the fish and sometimes even attracts fish.

Q: You're talking about dry flies, aren't you?

Roos: Yes, I'm talking about dry flies, but I'll do the same thing with a nymph. When you've got depth it's even more important to power mend rather than cast again because it takes time to get that fly back down again. So why not go ahead and move that fly four feet your way but get the line back upstream?

Trout Unlimited

Q: Let me change directions a bit and ask about environmental issues and Trout Unlimited. What is your involvement these days with T.U.?

Roos: I've been a member of Trout Unlimited since 1967, but I got really actively involved in 1986 when we formed the Blackfoot Chapter of T.U. I'm a former president and vice-president of that chapter, and these days I'm president again. I've served on the state T.U. council for several years now. We've done a lot of co-operative projects up there with U.S. Fish and Wildlife Service, with the Montana Department of Fish, Wildlife and Parks and we also work closely with the Soil Conservation District and the Water Quality Bureau. They are co-operative projects with landowners.

Q: What, specifically, is T.U. doing about the Blackfoot?

Roos: The Montana Department of Fish, Wildlife and Parks found, when they began to study the Blackfoot to discover what the heck was wrong with it— why the fishing was going to pot—that the river had lost its lifeblood. The small and large tributaries of the Blackfoot had been impacted to the extent that the river didn't have its spawning and rearing habitat.

So, since 1989, we've been doing co-operative projects with landowners and with those agencies I mentioned. We've been very successful in fund raising. We're also advocates on the political scene. We're gravely concerned about the proposed 7-Up Pete Joint Venture, the large gold mine that's proposed for the headwaters of the Blackfoot. We've participated in cleaning up some acid mine drainage from five old mine sites in the Heddleston district.

The Blackfoot chapter of T.U. has been without a doubt a national leader in working with landowners, getting projects done and rehabilitating habitat.

Catch-and-Release

Q: How do you feel about catch-and-release?

Roos: I favor it, of course, but I think there's a middle ground. There are people out there who think it's a mortal sin to kill a fish now and then. But I think people ought to have the right to kill an occasional fish if they feel good about it. As recently as six or seven or so years ago we'd now and then let people

147

keep a couple of small fish to have for lunch along the river, but we decided that the fisheries couldn't handle it, even though it was just an occasional thing. But there are places where I don't think it hurts to take a few fish. It depends on the pressure and the health of the population. Another aspect of catch-and-release that's starting to become an issue is the animal rights folks saying that it's not right to catch fish, give them pain and then release them.

Q: Do they say don't catch them, or do they say if you catch them then kill them?
Roos: They're saying both. Some say you shouldn't fish and others say catch them only if you're going to eat them. It's an extension of the no-hunting concept. I can't predict whether that will be a major problem down the road, but I've got an answer to it if it does. That's the raise-and-release. Cut the hooks off at the bend and just fish for getting the fish to take the fly.

Q: How do you raise-and-release with a nymph?
Roos: You don't. But with streamers you could.

Whirling Disease
Q: What do you think about whirling disease?
Roos: I feel that there are two solutions to whirling disease: different species and a more resistant strain of the rainbow. Brown trout seem to be more resistant to it than rainbows. We don't know how susceptible some of the other species are. Whitefish don't seem to be susceptible. Cutthroats are, they think. So the whirling disease is a major problem that Montana has right now. It deserves money and concentration of effort.

I try to run my life by not worrying about the things I don't have much control over and doing things about those things I do have control over. So I'm doing what I can about whirling disease, which is not much. And I'm not going to worry too much about it, either.

But it surely could have a devastating effect on the wild-trout sport-fishing industry in Montana. And it's doing that right now to the businesses on the Madison.

Q: How do you feel about the quality of fishing in your area?
Roos: I'd rather be here than anywhere, even than some other part of Montana. I had a chance to move to West Yellowstone, but I don't enjoy that because of the number of people there. It's just boat after boat, crazy life, and I don't think that's what fishing ought to be. That gets back to my tomahawk creeks idea. If I go down to the Missouri and there are too many boats I'll take off to one of my tomahawk creeks.

148

I have a lower sensitivity to crowded fishing conditions than most of my clients. But rather than raise their sensitivity to crowds, I try to raise their sensitivity to the other things you get when you go fishing other than catching a whole bunch of fish.

Stream-usage Regulation

Q: Speaking of overcrowding, do you think that stream usage should be regulated?

Roos:—Yes, I do. I think we have a growing river overcrowding problem in several areas around Montana, and I've been directly involved in resolving that issue. We've introduced a bill in each session of the state legislature from 1993 through 1997 which would have given the Department of Fish, Wildlife and Parks the authority to regulate conflicts on public waters in Montana. None of the bills got through both houses of the legislature, though.

Q: When you say "conflicts" do you mean conflicts among fishermen? What sort of conflicts?

Roos: We've got overcrowding of fishing water, we've got people getting on each other's nerves. These conflicts involve all kinds of recreationists on public waters, not just fishermen. On the Bighorn, for example, we've had fist-fights between fishermen and threats of more than that. It's all going to get worse, and we will eventually be forced to regulate those things.

Q: How would you regulate conflicts of that sort, other than with police officers patrolling the good stretches of water?

Roos: Empowering some state agency to monitor and control the social issues related to recreational use of public waters is the first thing, but it's just a first step. The next step would be regulating the types of use, and as a last resort regulating numbers. Which is what they do on the Smith River now.

In addition to being able to regulate who fishes where and when, there are less intrusive things they could do, such as say which stretches of a river are open or closed to power boats, which stretches are open to float planes and jet skis. In the Flathead and Bitterroot area they have float planes, jet skis and hover craft—and it's spreading all over.

Q: Do you think that the use of Montana waters by so many non-Montana fishermen poses any problems?

Roos: Yes, I do. The constantly increasing use of Montana rivers by out-of-staters is another stream-usage problem.

I believe that Montana sportsmen should have an opportunity to do what they love, to use their own home waters, and they're losing that. It's been documented on the Bighorn by Fish, Wildlife and Parks that for the last few years the percentage of non-locals has increased dramatically in the warmer seasons and the locals are now taking a larger percentage of the use in the colder weather. So it appears that the locals would rather fish and freeze as opposed to fish and fight other fishermen.

I think we have to deal with the out-of-stater problem, and I'm part of that problem. I'm an outfitter and I bring people in. I try to balance that moral dilemma with my efforts on behalf of resource issues and river overcrowding issues.

Regulating Outfitters

Q: What about regulating outfitters? Has anyone addressed that issue?

Roos:—Personally, I strongly favor regulating outfitters and guides, as well as regulating stream-usage by the public. And the Montana outfitting industry has supported this concept. It's been a difficult process over the past couple of years to get that support. Some years ago, I drew up a bill and had it introduced into the legislature, but it got downed by the outfitters pretty quickly. But now that kind of legislation has the support of both fishing outfitter organizations in the state, MOGA (Montana Outfitters and Guides Association) and FOAM (Fishing Outfitters Association of Montana). Regulating the outfitters has got to happen, but it won't work unless all recreationists are regulated as well.

Final Words of Wisdom

Q: How do your environmental views specifically affect what you do, and what you advocate that others do, out there on the water?

Roos: I advocate that fishermen, even experts, catch fewer fish, that they go for quality of experience rather than quantity of fish. You have to remember that every time a fish is caught it puts a lot of stress on him, and lessens his chance of survival. Also, when you catch-and-release a fish he's not going to be available for other fishermen to catch for a couple of days. When you spot a pod of fish on the Missouri, for instance, instead of seeing how many you can catch, try to catch the biggest one or the one in the most challenging position. If you spook the pod by catching him because he is on the far side, then, call it a day, move on to fish somewhere else, take a nap or go watch birds for a while.